Take steps to walk

The Twelve-Step program of Alcoholics Anonymous has helped millions of people conquer alcoholism. In *Anyone Anonymous*, Tim Timmons shows how these tried-and-true steps can be applied to *any* kind of problem you may face in life. He offers a biblically sound plan of recovery through reliance on Jesus Christ as your Higher Power. "The Seven Deadlies"— pride, greed, lust, gluttony, envy, resentment, laziness — are introduced as the prevalent character flaws that can manifest themselves as stubborn, destructive habits. Incorporating Alcoholics Anonymous steps into *Anyone Anonymous* steps, Timmons shows how you can:

- **'Fess up**—face your problem with God's help (are you a "Stuckor," "Stuckee," or a co-dependent?)
- **Look up** — resign your position as God and reclaim your life by turning yourself over to Him
- **Clean up** — take moral inventory, and completely confess to God and others
- **Give up**—let God change you through His grace and the truth of His Word
- **Straighten up**—mend relationships, past and present — forgive and be forgiven
- **Keep it up**—avoid and deal with relapses

Anyone Anonymous will help you overcome the problems that are keeping you "stuck in life." Now you can break free from addictive or compulsive behaviors. You'll experience recovery through discovery, as you enjoy a newly found sense of self-esteem.

BY Tim Timmons
Maximum Marriage
Hooked on Life
Call It Love or Call It Quits
Anyone Anonymous

ANYONE
ANONYMOUS

TIM TIMMONS

Fleming H. Revell Company
Old Tappan, New Jersey

Unless otherwise identified, Scripture quotations in this book are from the New American Standard Bible, © The Lockman Foundation 1960, 1962, 1963, 1968, 1971, 1972, 1973, 1975, 1977.
Scripture quotations identified AT are the author's translation.
Material from Francis A. Schaeffer's *He Is There and He Is Not Silent* © 1972 by Francis A. Schaeffer. Used by permission of Tyndale House Publishers,Inc. All rights reserved.

Library of Congress Cataloging-in-Publication Data

Timmons, Tim.
    Anyone anonymous / Tim Timmons.
       p.   cm.
    Includes bibliographical references.
    ISBN 0-8007-5351-8
    1. Self-actualization (Psychology)—Religious aspects—
Christianity.   2. Interpersonal relations—Religious aspects—
Christianity.   3. Twelve-step programs.   I. Title.
BV4598.2.T55   1990
248.8'6—dc20   90-30959
                                                                    CIP

Copyright © 1990 by Tim Timmons
Published by the Fleming H. Revell Company
Old Tappan, New Jersey 07675
Printed in the United States of America

TO
the people of South Coast
Community Church, whose willingness
to share their struggles provided
the inspiration for this book.

Special thanks to:

Diane Johnson, for her research and
editorial assistance on this project.

Bonnie Vaillancourt, for coordinating
my hectic schedule and for typing the
manuscript.

Contents

Introduction

In June 1935, two fellow strugglers, Bill W., a New York stockbroker, and Dr. Bob, an Akron physician, learned what it takes to effectively help each other remain clean and sober. Through personal trial and error and a Power greater than themselves, they were able to compose one of the most powerful documents ever written—the Twelve Steps. No tool or program has been created to equal its effectiveness in aiding the recovery of alcoholics! This is not based upon biased opinion, but on a simple reading of the facts. Treatment centers, the world of medicine, the various religious institutions, and virtually every school of therapy must all bow to the powerful dynamics of Alcoholics Anonymous and its Twelve Steps to Recovery. The reason is extremely pragmatic: It works! The Twelve Steps are simply profound.

Over the years, the Twelve Steps through the Anonymous group programs have been effectively expanded into other problem areas. For eating disorders there is Overeaters Anonymous. For the problem of drugs there is Cocaine Anonymous and Narcotics Anonymous. For the families of addicts and substance abusers there is Al-Anon. For the children of addicts and substance abusers there is ACA (Adult Children of Alcoholics). In addition to the various substance addictions and abuses there are several other uses of the Twelve Steps, for example with compulsive gambling, sexual addictions, and so on.

Observing the growing interest and the expanded application of the Twelve Steps into all kinds of addiction areas, it became very clear to me that there was no problem area out of their reach. It's not just for the addictions of our world, but for every conceivable problem man faces! Personal problems—phobias, depression, self-esteem, lying, resentment and bitterness, guilt, handicaps (physical, emotional, and mental), abuse. Relational problems—marital, dating, friendships, conflicts in general, divorce, parental, victimization, loneliness, loss of loved ones. Vocational problems—financial, out of work, dissatisfaction, mistreatment, being fired, bankruptcy. Now, I prescribe the Twelve Steps for every problem I face in the counseling room.

The real test was when I began to work through the Twelve Steps on my own. There are not enough seminars, workshops, books, tapes, or personal therapy sessions to produce the positive, life-changing results I gained through the Steps! You, too, can have this life-changing experience if you will work the Steps.

I have found—both personally and professionally—no greater vehicle to launch people into the process of healing those who hurt than these Twelve Steps:

1. We admitted that we were powerless over alcohol—that our lives had become unmanageable.
2. Came to believe that a Power greater than ourselves could restore us to sanity.

3. Made a decision to turn our will and our lives over to the care and direction of God as we understood Him.

4. Made a searching and fearless moral inventory of ourselves.

5. Admitted to God, to ourselves, and to another human being the exact nature of our wrongs.

6. Were entirely ready to have God remove all these defects of character.

7. Humbly asked Him to remove our shortcomings.

8. Made a list of all persons we had harmed, and became willing to make amends to them all.

9. Made direct amends to such people wherever possible, except when to do so would injure them or others.

10. Continued to take personal inventory and when we were wrong promptly admitted it.

11. Sought through prayer and meditation to improve our conscious contact with God as we understood Him, praying only for knowledge of His will for us and the power to carry that out.

12. Having had a spiritual awakening as the result of these steps, we tried to carry this message to alcoholics, and to practice these principles in all our affairs.*

* The Twelve Steps reprinted with permission of Alcoholics Anonymous World Services, Inc. Adaptations of this material throughout the book with permission.

The Twelve Steps have been miraculously effective for millions of people in the midst of a multitude of problems. And by word of mouth this brief, but lethal list of principles continues to spread to those who are seeking help with their painful problems. It's been a life-changing experience for millions. It can be a life-changing experience for you and those you love most.

Part I
Fess Up!

Step #1   *We admitted that we were powerless over our problem—that our lives had become unmanageable.*

Step #2   *We came to believe that a Power greater than ourselves could restore us to sanity.*

1
Problems and
Pain

Many years ago I heard a story that vividly describes the condition in which most people find themselves. There was a man by the name of Jones who was a proud owner of a Volkswagen Bug, but it was in the shop most of the time. This was not a problem to Jones since he viewed himself as an amateur mechanic. Whenever he took his car in for servicing, he was right there giving advice on what should be done. He *loved* the experience. The mechanic dreaded it.

On one particular day when Jones brought his VW in for repair, the mechanic, already exasperated as a result of a very stressful morning, was pushed over the edge at the sight of Jones coming. He threw down his wrench in disgust, walked toward Jones, and said, "Jones, I'll fix your car today, but you have to remain right here behind this white line. I simply can't handle your conversation today."

The mechanic jumped into the car and drove it into the

garage, but through the rearview mirror he could see that Jones was trotting right behind him. As always, Jones was coming to offer his opinion concerning the mechanical problem of his car. "Jones, I asked you nicely not to follow me. Since you have anyway, I've got a great idea. Come over here." The mechanic took him over to the side about thirty feet away from his car. Then he drew a circle all around where Jones was standing and said, "I bet you can't stay inside this circle while I work on your car." Jones responded, "Hey, this is terrific—a game? I've never played this before! Let's do it!" and stood at attention in the middle of the circle.

The enraged mechanic went over to his tool bench, picked up a huge sledgehammer, and walked over to Jones's car. As the mechanic raised the sledgehammer over the VW as if to smash it, he glanced at Jones to see what he might be thinking at this moment. Much to his surprise Jones was standing in the circle with a mischievous smirk on his face. That did it! The mechanic was furious! He came down on top of Jones's little car with one strong blow. WHAP! He looked up only to see Jones still standing in the circle, but his smirk had been transformed into laughter. This sent the mechanic into a complete rage! He began beating Jones's car as hard as he could until he was near exhaustion. As the mechanic's energy wore down Jones was still in the circle, but he wasn't standing. Jones was now on the ground, laughing himself silly and holding his sides! The mechanic went berserk! He really lost it! He beat and beat on that car until he had successfully leveled it to about a six-inch plane.

When the mechanic saw that Jones was still inside the circle and laughing harder than ever, he picked up his sledgehammer and walked over to Jones. "I have totally destroyed your car, and you're over here inside this circle laughing like a hyena! Tell me, Jones, what's so funny?" Because he was laughing so hard, Jones could hardly speak. Finally he got it out: "While you were beating up on my car, I stepped out of the circle three times!"

Now, Jones had a problem. He was playing games while something very serious was going on, much like the people in our world today. Too many people are playing games while something very serious is going on.

Problems   We all have them. No one is exempt from them. Our problems vary greatly. Some problems are so small we stumble over them. Others serve as obstacles to what we really want. Still others become overwhelming; they control our lives so that our lives become unmanageable. This is what is commonly known as *stuck!*

In a previous book, *Hooked on Life*, we demonstrated the different problems that can get us stuck: alcohol, drugs, workaholism, food, disease, molestation, divorce, relationships, rebellion, anger, guilt, phobias, handicaps, loneliness, and so on.

When we examine these problems, some of them—such as alcohol and drug abuse—seem to be the worst and carry the greatest stigma. Others—such as deadly disease, and physical and mental handicaps—seem to be a result of victimizing attacks against humanity. The less obvious yet most common causes of being stuck are compulsive work, hidden spouse or child abuse, divorce for convenience, impulsive affairs, disguised loneliness, smoking. We rarely consider these to be desperate problems. But they are, and you definitely *can* get stuck in them!

Problems are part of the human condition. And because of the pain that accompanies these problems, we naturally tend to turn to chemicals, activities, and people in an unhealthy way. This is precisely the point of becoming *hooked*

or addicted—overly dependent upon something or someone. We will attach ourselves to *anything* in order to alleviate or postpone the pain. So we become chemically
dependent, behaviorally *dependent*, or relationally *dependent*
to some degree!

Answers   Practical and real down-to-earth answers
are extremely difficult to find. Answers are what we have
for other people's problems but not our own. As one har-
ried homemaker sighed, "I have so many problems that if
something terrible happened to me it would be at least
two weeks before I could get around to doing anything
about it!" Authentic answers can only be realized through
the process of methodically working through them. There
has never been a more productive system for personal
problem solving than the Twelve Steps of Alcoholics
Anonymous. No matter what your problem is, you can
solve it by working with these dynamic steps. Define your
problem or problems and carefully work them through,
step by step. To do otherwise is playing games with your
life, and a life is a terrible thing to waste!

Don't wait—Do it now!

Step #1   *We admitted that we were powerless over
our problem—that our lives had become
unmanageable.*

Step #2   *We came to believe that a Power greater
than ourselves could restore us to sanity.*

The first two steps of the Twelve Steps deal with the
problems we all possess personally and with those we
perceive in people around us. The urge is to fix them, but
I want to demonstrate how impossible such a task is—no
matter how hard we try! In order to prove this point, we
must view the problems we own and those that we observe in a fourfold way:

1. Realize the existence of the dysfunctional families,
2. understand the resulting disturbances created by the dysfunctional families,
3. see the need to deal with the resistance and rationalizations made in order to avoid facing the problems, and
4. believe that the only life-oriented option available for recovery is to make that first, most critical decision!

I.   Reality: Dysfunctional Families

Neighbors: The Stuckees and the Stuckors

As I mentioned previously, when problems arise, pain is an inevitable result. And since most human beings are resistant to pain, anything that will serve to alleviate the pain is welcomed. The "anything" is anything that will bring about some kind of temporary, fast pain relief. The list of anythings is almost infinite. Some people drink to relieve the pain. Some use drugs for relief. Others eat or smoke, become hypercritical, act out with sexual promiscuity or a compulsion for pornography, lie, and so on. The anythings that are used for relief only serve to postpone the pain and the problem. In fact, there is such a tight attachment to these anythings that many times they become habitual, even addictive. This condition is what I call *stuck!*

To some degree we are all into this cycle of problem → pain → postponement of pain → addiction. Now picture a family with each member struggling to postpone (run away from or avoid) his or her personal problems. This reality is the primary obstacle that prevents the family unit from operating constructively. A nonconstructive family unit is destructive or what is known as *dysfunctional*.

Dysfunctional families are everywhere. The more I counsel people and study life, the more convinced I am that everyone emerges from a dysfunctional family—everyone! In this imperfect world, people simply do not play out their roles properly or perfectly. These role failures merge to create the dystunctional family with all of its actions and reactions.

People constantly say things like, "I know that my dad loved me—in his own way. He never really said it; we weren't a touchy-feely family. But I know he really loved me." The aching pain of not having love validated by a parent is indelible. Your family—whether highly dysfunctional or not—has marked you in some way. This mark becomes apparent in the roles and games you learn to play in order to cope with life's problems—coping to avoid as much pain as possible.

Your coping methods may not seem so bad until all of the costs are added up. Every time you decide to postpone pain you also put off facing the problem. Fortunately for us all, some of these problems will go away without any attention from us. But there are far too many problems that stubbornly refuse to fade away. There is a very critical principle that comes into play here: **Face the problem now and avoid the disaster later, or avoid the problem now and face the disaster later.** The balloon payment that builds as you postpone the pain and the problem is more than you'll ever want to pay! This is how we all become *stuck*.

It is helpful to know what stuck is and how it happens, and then to realize you can't get unstuck until you understand how you stay stuck. The best way to view how a person can remain stuck over long periods of time is to take a look at two very close neighbors. I call them the Stuckees and the Stuckors. You see, for every person who is stuck (the Stuckees) there are all kinds of people ready and willing to assist in keeping him stuck (the Stuckors). For every person who has an alcohol problem, there is a Stuckor out there who is offering him another drink. For every person with a drug problem, there is somebody out there inviting him to another party. For every person who has an eating problem, someone is making brownies!

The interesting thing about these neighbors is that one cannot survive without the other. The Stuckors are the enablers in our world. They lead the Stuckees to believe that they are all right, that their problem isn't that bad, and that there is no need for any drastic change. The Stuckors do most of their enabling by silently putting up with an otherwise intolerable situation. The Stuckors are known as "saints" for putting up with the Stuckees for so long and in such a kind way. People are amazed at how patient and loving the Stuckors can be. But let me assure you that the Stuckors are not playing the role of saints in the lives of the Stuckees, because their actions are not helpful and healing but harmful and hurting. They continually allow the Stuckees to slowly destroy themselves without any caring confrontation. Why? Take away the Stuckee and the Stuckor no longer has a role in life. No more Mr. Nice Guy; no more saintliness. But there is more to it than that.

The Stuckee, most likely, is not going anywhere on his own. Being human, he too has areas of stuckness where he is in dire need of a Stuckor. So it is in most Stuckee/Stuckor relationships that the Stuckee and the Stuckor switch roles for each other. If you don't tell me that I drink too much, I won't hassle you about your overeating. It's a pact. You tell me I'm OK and I'll tell you that you're OK.

Family Album: The Stuckee and the Stuckor

The Stuckees and the Stuckors are such good neighbors that they frequently move in together and live as families. Their family album serves as a mirror for the rest of us. There are five pages to this family album, and each page tells a revealing story.

Page 1—Mr. Stuckee and Mrs. Stuckor   Even though each member of the family is a Stuckee, let's take a profile of one of them and observe how every other family member responds to him. The entire family moves almost in unison. Mr. Stuckee, the husband/dad, is stuck in alcoholism, but doesn't acknowledge his problem in any way. He is into a strong denial about his problem, even though it has been pointed out to him several times by others. Mrs. Stuckor, the wife/mom, helps her husband to remain in his stuck position. She enables him to continue drinking by joining him in his denial. "You didn't drink that much last night. I know you can stop anytime you want to. Besides, I don't think your problem is that bad."

On the surface she aids in his denial, but underneath she is seething with anger to the point of resentment. On the outside she appears to be terrific, but on the inside she is ticked! From time to time this resentment slips out—especially behind closed doors. She desperately wants to keep her "knight in shining armor" shiny, but she also finds herself near the boiling point most of the time. It's impossible to stay under control all of the time. Her children are watching. They see it all—the protective denial as well as the deep resentment. They can sense a serious problem brewing that could easily destroy their family.

Out of desperation each child moves into some kind of survival mode in response to the problem.

Page 2—The Family Hero   This page of the family album presents the child whose survival mode is to achieve the status of life necessary to save the family name. He knows the family problems are desperate and someone must do something dramatic to save and protect the family from disaster or embarrassment.

The Family Hero is driven to excel in everything. His is a compulsion to achieve—to press for peak performance. The Family Heroes are the workaholics of our world. They must be the best at everything they attempt to do. Although their effort is noble, it doesn't succeed in solving the initial problem within the family.

Page 3—The Scapegoat   The third page of the family album shows the child who survives by turning attention away from the parents' problem and toward his own immediate problem. This problem may take the form of sexual promiscuity, pregnancy, chemical abuse, or some sort of battle with the authorities. The community sympathizes with the parents about the child's problem, completely overlooking the primary problem, which is that of the parents. When this happens, the almost unconscious strategy of the scapegoat has proven effective.

The most interesting thing about the scapegoat is that in his attempt to divert attention away from Mom and Dad's problem he has now become Stuckee Number Two, setting off a new chain of reaction throughout the entire family. Remember for every Stuckee there is a Stuckor. This occurs repeatedly throughout the family!

Page 4—The Comic   On page 4 the family album pictures the child who uses humor to divert attention away from the problem of the parents. He reasons, "It's better to laugh than to cry, so laugh it off!'' Fun and games are used to mask the real pain that is felt so deeply.

Page 5—The Lost Child   The final page of the Stuckee/Stuckor family album portrays the child whose survival mode is to withdraw from the family—from everyone! This is the loner. He is not a troublemaker in any way, but he is often in the deepest trouble of all. All his trouble has been internalized and held inside. It's just easier to withdraw than to face the pain of the problem he senses. This is the child who will most likely not marry and too many times die early. His parents often comment, ''We've never had any difficulty with him at all—not even a peep.'' But, in this case, that is exactly the problem: He hasn't made a peep in years! In a sense, he hasn't officially entered the human race yet.

The Stuck Family Album tells an interesting story about the family as a whole and each individual within the family. The family is *in balance*, but each individual is *out of joint!* There is a relatively new but extremely popular term for this complex problem. The term is *codependency*. Melody Beattie, author of the excellent book *Codependent No More*, defines codependency as follows: ''A codependent person is one who has let another person's behavior affect him or her, and who is obsessed with controlling that person's behavior.''[1] Originally, this term was used to describe the person or persons whose lives were affected as a result of their being involved with someone who was chemically dependent. The codependent spouse or child or lover was seen as having developed a pattern of coping with life that was not healthy, as a reaction to someone else's drug or alcohol abuse. But now it is viewed as much broader in its scope, including adult children of alcoholics; people in relationships with emotionally or mentally disturbed persons; people in relationships with chronically ill people; parents of children with behavior problems; people in relationships with irresponsible people; professionals—nurses, social workers, and others in the "helping" occupations. Even recovering alcoholics and addicts noticed they were codependent and perhaps had been long before becoming chemically dependent. In a nutshell, codependency is a set of "self-defeating, learned behaviors or character defects that result in a diminished capacity to initiate or to participate in loving relationships."[2]

I am seeing this in epidemic proportions in the counseling room today. Marriages are absolutely blowing apart as one or both partners stifle their emotions until either the emotions themselves explode or the person explodes. Their codependency over the years has only allowed them to react to the other's feelings, rather than to act out or initiate their own personal feelings until finally the suffocation is so great that in order for there to be any kind of survival, a dramatic and desperate move must be made. That move happens when one partner announces, "I'm moving out! I've had it! I want a divorce!"

But the heart of the definition of codependency is not in the other person upon whom we have overly focused. It lies in ourselves, in the ways we have let other people's behavior affect us and in the ways we try to affect them. It's a habitual system of thinking, feeling, and behaving toward ourselves and others that can cause us great pain. These behaviors and habits are self-destructive. We frequently react to people who are destroying themselves; we react by learning to destroy ourselves. These habits can lead us into, or keep us in, destructive relationships—relationships that don't work. These behaviors can sabotage relationships that may otherwise have worked. These behaviors can prevent us from finding peace and happiness with the most important person in our lives—

ourselves. And these behaviors belong to the only person
each of us can control or change—*ourselves!*[3]

As individuals we are stuck and so we get into all sorts
of unhealthy dependencies. As families we are individuals
stuck together with other stuck people—each one entering
into various coping responses. Each person's goal in life is
to survive, not really to live life in the best, most fulfilled
way possible. Now we really have a problem—we all need
one another in order to keep our weird coping responses
and our out-of-focus dependencies going. In other words,
we—and all our problems—are vitally linked to one another. If I am going to continue nourishing my problem, I
need you to continue nourishing yours. We are not only
linked to one another as Stuckors and Stuckees, many of
us are also linked in a codependency. A codependent relationship is one in which the nonaddict is overly focused
upon the addict—almost tied to the other person's mood
and behavior. When you are hinged emotionally with another person, especially an addict, you are not your own
person and cannot develop into a healthy, fulfilled human
being.

II. Results: Disturbances

Individual dependencies, family coping responses, and
relational codependencies can all trigger life-destructive
disturbances within each individual. In most cases, we
don't become immobilized by these disturbances, but we
all have the "rough edges" that hold us back from fulfilling our potential and block our relationships from the
growth we all desire. We do everything possible to cover
these rough edges or to suppress and repress them so that
they are buried and put behind us. But as John Powell has
so aptly stated: "When you repress those things which

you don't want to live with, you don't really solve the problem, because you don't bury the problem dead, you bury it alive. It remains alive and active inside of you."[4]

You definitely can bury your problems, but they will not die in this buried state. They will continue to fester and frustrate you so that you cannot live your life as it was intended to be lived. These are the results of our dysfunctional world. I call these results the *disturbances* within each individual. There are, at least, three results or disturbances within us:

1. Personal dissatisfaction
2. People detachment
3. A destination sickness as far as purpose

Personal Dissatisfaction

The first and primary result of our dysfunctional world is the intense, personal dissatisfaction we live with. The more I meet with people from all over the world and all walks of life, the clearer it becomes to me how unhappy people really are. There is a desperation within—a lack of optimism. There is a deep sense of dissatisfaction with personal matters, marriages, relationships in general, children, vocations, government, religion, and on and on. It's a dissatisfaction with life—with *who we are!*

A simple way to verify this dissatisfaction is to note the thousands of advertisements and what each one promises to deliver. No matter how differently it is expressed— whether it be for toothpaste, beer, cigarettes, perfume, automobiles, clothes, homes, vacation resorts, seminars, workshops, or candy bars—the message (explicit or implicit) always carries with it the promise of happiness and satisfaction. Why is every corporation spending millions in dollars and energy to sell their products by promising happiness or satisfaction if their product is bought? The answer is too obvious. The supply is desperately low and the demand is extremely high. We don't possess satisfaction! And the vacuum created in our guts is too real and too painful. That vacuum exists, because of our inability to trust or place faith in anything or anyone.

People Detachment

The second disturbance is people detachment. We know painfully little of the warmth and security of intimacy within relationships. In fact, we have become the masters of the "surfacey" relationship. Daily we move through our world with, "Hi! How are you? How are the kids? . . . your business? . . . your car? . . . your house?" And we call these surfacey conversations relationships! But they are nothing more than sharing a few facts and niceties that will never progress into a personal relationship. It's safer that way.

This may be the most gut-wrenching emotional struggle we face as humans. On the one hand, we urgently want and need to be connected with another live person—to love and be loved. But on the other hand, when the opportunity arises, we run away from the possibility in fear. We act as if the intimacy it could create might possibly destroy us.

How many times have you thought about expressing some action of love toward another—a touch, a kind word, a hug, a time to talk—and just as quickly as the thought crossed your mind, you dismissed it. "He wouldn't understand. What's the use? It won't help anyway. I'll look stupid or it'll be too awkward." This sort of self-talk is quite effective in bringing us to a screeching halt *before* we carry out an intimate expression of love toward another. Just when the possibility of connecting or bonding with another human being presents itself, there is this little mechanism that throws up a shield. It's a shield that *protects* us from the very thing we need most—to *belong*, to be attached! So we remain detached—protected from the pain of living within relationships and "protected" from the promise of life that only relationships can provide. This is another destructive result of the dysfunctional world in which we live. It's another vacuum in the gut. This time the vacuum has been created by our inability to give and receive love in a sustained relationship.

Purpose/Destination Sickness

The third destructive result of our dysfunctional world is a purposelessness—a kind of destination sickness. This is a sense of not feeling worthwhile. It's a lack of significance or making an impact on the world—*any* impact that matters to another human being. Who cares if I live or die? Why am I here? Where am I going with my life? What difference does my life make?

These questions become increasingly haunting to the point of dull depression. Since the present has little personal significance and the future promises to be only a continuation of the present, there is not much to look forward to. It's like a downward spiral. The personal dissatisfaction and the people detachment move us to a hopelessness. The inner vacuum here is created by the inability to have a sense of destiny—a hope for the future.

The reality? Problems! No one is exempt. We all suffer from the problems that are produced by our dysfunctional world. To some degree all of us have been or are being affected by this dysfunctional world.

The results? Pain! The pain that we suffer because of our problems is also universal. To some degree all of us know the pain of personal dissatisfaction, people detachment, and destination sickness.

Now, how do we fix the problems and the pain?

2
Resistance and Recovery

Since the problems and resulting pain hurt so much, there is a passionate search for any possible way to *fix it*. Notice that I didn't use the word *solve*, because for the most part it is not an intense search to solve the problems that cause the pain. On the contrary, there seems to be a real resistance to doing the kinds of things that would solve the problem over the long haul. The passionate search is for any way to fix it so that the problem and the pain disappear immediately. There are basically three common ways of doing this.

Relieve the Pain

This method is a quick fix: Do whatever you can to handle the problem or the pain precipitated by the problem with a fast remedy of some kind. It's a "snake-oil" kind of method. Most people will do anything to get some fast, temporary pain relief—even if the action buries them deeper into their problem! So, the alcoholic drinks; the drug addict snorts, smokes, pops a pill, or shoots up; the food addict either binges or purges or both; the sex addict acts out some sexual fantasy or desire; the liar lies again; the gambler gambles once more. In other words, people in search of the quick fix will retreat to acting out the core problem that causes their pain in the first place. They reason that they'll do it (whatever it is) one more time, and then, no more.

You see, if your goal is pain relief, you are already in trouble. But it's difficult to live in this society without acquiring this kind of orientation. The marketing of "painless products" is everywhere: You can reshape your body and lose weight—painlessly! You can purchase a car, boat, or house—painlessly! You can enjoy sex with anyone you choose tonight—painlessly! You can be successful and fulfilled—painlessly! You can divorce your mate—painlessly! You can live beyond your circumstances and the obstacles that come your way—painlessly! But there is one major problem with respect to the many offers that bombard your ears, eyes, and mailboxes—they don't work! Life cannot be fixed so that you are relieved of all pain.

There is no quick fix that will provide temporary relief of pain without causing greater problems in the long run. Relief of pain will not accomplish what we really need. Instead, there must be a way of resolving the problem that causes the pain.

Repair Other People

The second way of fixing the pain is to repair other people. This method diverts the attention away from you and toward the world around you. It's much easier to focus on the failures of other people rather than to face your own desperation, to preach rather than practice. I had a close friend who used this form of projecting his own problems on others. You could sense it coming. Whenever he failed at something, you knew someone was going to receive a lecture on something *they* had failed to do! If you can make enough noise fixing the people around you, soon you will be known as the "fixer of people" and not one who needs any help yourself. Although there are many good reasons people enter the helping professions, far too many are there masking their own problems. That's why you'll hear weird stories that seem to contradict themselves—a marriage counselor who runs off with another man's wife; the minister, who is known for pounding the pulpit against pornography, but who is caught using it for his own personal pleasure; the drug counselor abusing drugs himself; the special agent known for outstanding service in catching drug dealers who is arrested for dealing on the side.

This is not a special plague among the helping professions, but seems to be a very real part of the human condition. We humans are riddled with contradictions in our life-styles, and we frequently choose to fix or cover our own problems by pointing out the problems in most of our friends and family and in all of our enemies. There's a natural tendency in all of us to blame and point the finger at someone else. Somehow it makes us feel a little better if we can lower someone a few notches. It's comforting to know that others have so many faults. But while we are busy pointing out the faults of others or suggesting ways to change them, our problems remain right where they are. They simply continue to fester within us. In other words, repairing other people will not fix us either.

Rationalize the Problem

In our attempts to fix it, relieving the pain and repairing other people account for how *most* of us handle our problems, but rationalizing the problem accounts for the way *all* of us attempt to fix it. This fix is the most universal of all. In fact, the dysfunctional world in which we live and the disturbances (dissatisfaction-detachment-destination sickness) produced are actually a minor part of our problems. Our biggest problem of all is our rationalizations— *denial!*

No one is exempt from this major cover-up. We all rationalize or deny everything we can about our negative side. This is not new; denial has been part of our nature since Adam and Eve initiated it in the Garden! Much of our denial is motivated by false perceptions that we have convinced ourselves are absolutely true. These unrealistic, negative perceptions just pop into our minds—*If I ever even open my mouth about this problem, I'll lose my job, my family will reject me, everyone will think I am nuts, dumb, or just plain stupid!*—and help us build our "great wall of denial."

Two of the most common denials or rationalizations are heard on the lips of everyone you know. The first is, "My problem is not that bad yet." This is common because we can think of any number of people who are worse off than we are. Now, think about this response. How bad does your problem have to be before you will do anything about it? Will it take a tragic accident? A broken relationship? A crippling disease? The loss of your job? Your family? A loved one? A death? *Just how bad does your problem have to get?*

The second most common denial is, "I can handle it myself." My only response to this one is, "If you could've, you would've!" The truth is since you can't handle this problem on your own, you won't. It's not enough that we are all experts in the art of denial, but we stick together in denial and help one another do it even better.

Don't Fix It—Don't Even Try

After years of counseling and grappling with people's problems, I am convinced that our greatest problem is that we actually *believe* we are able to fix ourselves. Let me offer you one of the most important pieces of information you will ever hear—*you can't fix yourself!* You can't do it. And it's in the trying that you create more problems and life becomes even more painful. You can't *fix* yourself, but you can and must *face* yourself and your problems. In my book *Hooked on Life*, we offered a piece of Texas wisdom: "If one person calls you a horse, ignore him. It's ridiculous! If two people call you a horse, you might check your hoofs or look in the mirror! But if three people call you a horse, you better buy a saddle!" If more than one person has said, "You've got a problem!" then it is very likely you have a problem and it's time to do something about it.

Not long ago a married couple sat in my office laying out the problems that had motivated them to seek counseling. There was nothing different about this marital battle, but there was a problem that repeatedly came up in our conversation. The issue of the husband's alcohol consumption was raised at least four times. His response was that his drinking had nothing to do with the problems in the marriage. He was in deep denial. His wife was negatively affected by his drinking, his two children were being negatively affected by his drinking, and his job performance was suffering because of his drinking. All of the evidence was in. His drinking was indeed a problem!

Once you gather evidence on yourself and you are al-

most ready to admit that you have a problem, you're ready
to listen to another piece of Texas wisdom: "When your
horse is dead, get off!" It sounds simple, but it is very
profound. When what you are doing in life isn't getting
you where you really want to go, you just may be riding a
dead horse. What a picture. So many people beating a
dead horse and hoping in vain to get where they want to
go. A dead horse will get you nowhere!

Everybody's got a problem. You can't fix it, but you
must face it. There is an interesting proverb written by
King Solomon centuries ago which set forth a vital principle for living life: "He who conceals or hides his failures
[problems] will not prosper." The reverse of this is also
true: He who openly confesses his failures [problems] *will*
prosper. No matter how effective your systems of fixing it
(relieving-repairing-rationalizing) are, you still must do
something about your problems or they will do you in.
You can't fix it—don't even try!

You Can't Fix It—Fess Up

You can't get fixed until you *Fess Up*. There must be a
starting point, and this is the best place to start. I am
convinced that this is the *only* place to start. In recovery
circles of all kinds you'll hear a terrific line: "You are as
sick as your secrets." Our sicknesses *are* our secrets. So,
face your secrets and Fess Up! There are three levels that
I suggest for fessing up:

Level #1—Be Aware   You must have some general
awareness of the dysfunctional contribution to your life,
the disturbances caused by this contribution, and the great
force of denial that moves within all of us. But, more important, you must face your own, personal problem or

problems. Remember the first two steps of the Twelve Steps:

#1 *We admitted that we were powerless over our problem—that our lives had become unmanageable.*

#2 *We came to believe that a Power greater than ourselves could restore us to sanity.*

There are at least three dimensions of awareness concerning your problem. The first is that you must be aware that you have a problem. But to stop here is to miss the point and will not get you anywhere. The second dimension is that you must be aware that you are powerless over your problem. You do not have the power to handle your problem by yourself—you are powerless to do anything effectively to solve it.

Now, if you are basically a normal person, you are probably arguing with me. The silent sentences usually flood the mind saying, *I am not powerless over my problem. I can handle it!* Try if you must, but you will have to return to this point in order to really solve the problem you are struggling with.

Third, you must be aware that your life is becoming or has become unmanageable. You have lost your job, damaged relationships, experienced financial disaster, lost your health, or any combination of these. You have a problem, you are powerless to solve it on your own, and your life has become unmanageable because of your problem.

Unmanageability can be extremely deceptive! It's been my experience that very few people are able to identify on their own how their lives have become unmanageable. Usually it has to be pointed out by friends, family, a counselor, or through some helpful tool like a book, film, or tape.

Just a few weeks ago I was counseling with a young couple concerning their marital conflicts. During the session there was a brief and mild comment by the woman about her husband's stock of "nudie magazines and videos." He seemed to be a little touchy about her remark, but calmly denied what she said, passing it off as "nothing at all."

After hearing their stories, I decided to go back to the magazine and video comment. Over the years I've discovered that under little comments like that lie the most critical issues in the relationship. When I asked him to tell me about the extent of his use of magazines and videos, he brushed it off as an old "beef" his wife had thrown up to him for years.

"It's nothing! So I like to look at a couple of girlie magazines and I like to watch a sexy video from time to time. So what?" As I pushed him to define "from time to time," he opened up as to how many purchases he made per month. His list of magazines, videos, and a subscription to pornographic materials sent to a post office box totaled an expenditure of $300 to $375 per month! The total even shocked him. His salary was $2,000 per month. Well over 15 percent of his monthly income was going down the pornographic drain. His two children were badly in need of clothes and medical assistance, and his marriage was on the brink of blowing apart. Was his life unmanageable? Just like most people he said, "No way!" But after closer examination, it was clear that his life was absolutely out of control. *Be aware of your problem!*

Level #2—Admit It   It's one thing to be aware that you have a problem, that you are powerless over it, and that your life has become unmanageable because of the problem. But it's so much more for you to *admit* the problem as yours. There's something about admitting to a personal problem that necessitates a tangible action in order to be most effective. For quite some time I have been using a simple method in the counseling room as well as before thousands in a seminar setting which helps this step stick. Take out a pen and some paper. I want you to write down the *big one*—the biggest personal problem you are facing right now, the one you struggle with most. Don't write down the secondary problems; go for the big one. Just by writing it down you have made a great start in fessing up. We'll work through your personal big one together as we move through the Twelve Steps. Once you have written it down, fold it like a book and hold it in your hand as you finish reading this chapter. Now, let's move on to the next level in fessing up.

Level #3—Ask God for Help   Level #1—Be Aware— and level #2—Admit It—are applications of Step 1 of the Twelve Steps: *We admitted that we were powerless over our problem—that our lives had become unmanageable.* Level #3— Ask God for Help—is the application of Step 2: *We came to believe that a Power greater than ourselves could restore us to sanity.* Without a doubt this is the great power behind the effectiveness of the Twelve Step programs throughout the world. You must come to the place where you recognize that you can't solve your problem on your own, that you need a higher power to get you through it. This completes the fessing up.

At this point in time you don't need to identify what or who the higher power is; just test the higher power out by asking God for help. As one older man put it when he came to this level in his personal journey toward freedom, "I know I can't fix or control my problem, and I've certainly proved that I can't manage my life anymore. God, if You are there, I need Your help right now with my problem

and with my life!" Just a simple statement of prayer is all
that is necessary.

As you hold that big one in your hand try praying the
following prayer:

> God, here is my problem. I realize that I am
> powerless over this and that my life is unman-
> ageable as long as this problem is in my life. So
> God, I ask for Your help with my problem right
> now—that You might help me do whatever it
> takes to solve it. Restore me to my sanity! Amen.

There's an old story about a rabbi who was traveling to
his first congregation in old Russia. He hired a driver and
a horse and wagon to take him to this very remote village
where he would spend the next several years of his life. As
they were making their way to the village, they came to a
long, gradual incline. About halfway up this hill the driver
stopped and said, "My horse, Rifke, is getting pretty old.
I think it would be best if you got out and walked the rest
of the way up this hill." So, the rabbi hopped out and
walked beside the wagon as it slowly rolled up the hill.
Approximately two miles later there was another, steeper
hill. Again the driver, with much concern in his voice,
said, "You know, I think both of us better get out of the
wagon on this hill. Otherwise, Rifke may not make it."
Mile after mile and hill after hill, the rabbi and the driver
ended up walking more than half the way, and much of
the time they were both pushing the wagon as Rifke did
his best to pull his load!

They arrived at the village after an exhausting all-day
trip. As the rabbi was paying the driver what they had
agreed upon he said, "I know why I came, because I'm the
new rabbi in this village. I understand why you came,

because you are the driver who was to bring me here. But tell me, *why did we bring Rifke?"*

You need to remove some Rifkes from your life! Start by trashing the big Rifke you wrote on your paper. That's right, trash it! We'll continue to work on it throughout the remaining chapters.

Remember, you can't get fixed, until you Fess Up!

Part II
Look Up!

Step #3   *Made a decision to turn our will and our lives over to the care and direction of God as we understood Him.*

3
Resign as God

When I first presented the action-step Fess Up, I was speaking to over five thousand people. Since I had them right in front of me, I decided to have them actually write out their "biggies" on paper and trash them in some barrels I had prepared for them in the back of the auditorium. In the week following this presentation my personal assistant and I had the task of reading each one of them. This was a rare experience. It was like listening to five thousand people pour their hearts out. You could just feel the emotion that each piece of paper represented. Many of them moved me to tears as I imagined the pain that must be in the heart of this one or that one. It was an incredibly moving experience.

One observation I was able to make through this experience is that all of our problems are relative. Each person's biggie is relative as you compare it with another person's biggie. As I compared some of my problems with what that group was facing it was clear that my problems are not all that bad. Then again, some of my problems are much worse than many of theirs. Problems are relative. No matter how you slice it, if the problems are yours, they are pretty bad; other people's problems are not nearly as bad—to *you!*

This reminds me of the old man who was driving his truck down the road with a horse trailer in tow. A wild driver in a red sports car bolted around the curve ahead, hit the old man, and ran him off the road. It was an awful wreck! The old man and his truck ended up in the ditch on one side of the road, and the horse and trailer flipped into the ditch on the other side of the road.

Even though the young man in the sports car was obviously at fault, he and his lawyer decided to fight the old man in court. They felt like they had a good defense. During the trial, the defense attorney put the old man on the witness stand and began to interrogate him about the wreck. The attorney said, "Now look, in the accident report it is stated that at the time of the wreck you claimed repeatedly that you were OK. You made this very clear to the two policemen who arrived on the scene. And now you are claiming all kinds of personal damage—broken bones, neck and back injuries, and so on. Now, which testimony are we to believe? The one at the scene of the accident when you said, 'I'm OK! I'm OK!' or your present claims of personal damages? You just cannot have it both ways. It's either one way or the other."

The old man answered the attorney's question with great calm and confidence. He said, "Let me explain something to you. When the two policemen arrived on the scene of the accident, they first walked over to my horse in the ditch right across from me. One of them said to the other, 'Is that horse OK?' The other one answered, 'No!' At that point they both took out their guns and shot him dead! Then the two policemen walked across the road over to where I was lying. They looked at me and one of them said, 'Are you OK?' And I quickly and confidently responded, 'I'm OK! I'm OK!' "

All problems *are* relative when followed with the thought, *compared to what?* But no matter the comparison, *your problems are your problems*. No one else wants them! Therefore, it's very difficult to give them away. You just cannot fix them or get rid of them. But there is something you *can* do with these unique possessions: You can turn your problems into opportunities for personal growth and fulfillment by walking step by step through the most dynamic steps ever penned. I want to help you do just that.

In Part I—Fess Up! we walked through the first two of the Twelve Steps:

> Step #1   *We admitted that we were powerless over our problem—that our lives had become unmanageable.*
>
> Step #2   *We came to believe that a Power greater than ourselves could restore us to sanity.*

Now we come to the third step which naturally builds upon these first two:

> Step #3   *We made a decision to turn our will and our lives over to the care and direction of God as we understood Him.*

The first two say Fess Up and the third says Look Up! Turn your will and life over to the care and direction of God—Look Up! Before we look at what that means, let's look at what it does not mean.

Shelve Your Brain? No

Does turning your will and life over to the care and direction of God mean that you must shelve your brain? No way! On the contrary, this action of looking up will enable you to *use* your brain, not *lose* it. In fact, the person who is stuck in his problem is on automatic pilot—the brain is not in gear. The shelves of this world are crammed with brains that were meant to be used. Instead, they are either unused or abused!

Everyone who is controlled, managed, or overwhelmed by a problem has learned to selectively shelve the brain much of the time. The pressure is on from every front for you to shelve your brain to some extent. The political front sometimes hopes for this and even offers to think for us! Several educational fronts, which exist in order to promote and develop the use of the brain, actually encourage the shelving process—don't think, just believe. The religious front often requires and even glorifies it. The New Age Movement desperately needs it in order for their system to work. The entertainment media—TV, radio, movies— seem to count on it. But turning your will and life over to the care and direction of God requires the exact opposite. To Look Up does *not* mean to shelve the brain; to Look Up means to think!

Stifle Your Individuality? No

Does turning your will and life over to the care and direction of God mean that you must stifle your individuality? No way! On the contrary, the action of looking up will enable you to embrace your individuality not stifle it.

In a world where we are constantly pressed to conform or to make others conform to be like us, individuality is lost. Very few organizations or movements truly push you to express your unique, one-of-a-kind individuality. It's too threatening! Yet turning your will and life over to the care and direction of God will move you closer to this unique opportunity of being *you*.

Sacrifice Your Lifelong Desires? No

Does turning your will and life over to the care and direction of God mean that you must sacrifice your life-long desires? No way! There is a natural knee-jerk reaction inside the human being that says, "If I really want something or want to do something that would cause me great joy, it certainly is not something that God would want!" This rumor seems to have been a part of most cultures throughout the centuries. Therefore, in the name of God and for God's pleasure, all kinds of self-destructive behavior is practiced—asceticism that includes beating, cutting, starving, or some sort of brutal self-denial. Some have even gone to the ultimate extreme of human sacrifice of children and adults!

The decision to turn your will and life over to the care and direction of God should not trigger self-denial as its major theme. There is so much more involved. Your genuine lifelong desires are products of who you are. In fact, most of those desires down deep in your gut are God-given in the first place. So turning your will and life over to the care and direction of God does not call for a massive and dramatic sacrifice of your lifelong desires. All who are able to take this great step of looking up seem to discover that they do what they really *want* to do in their lives. It's true that in many cases, the "want" is changed, but they have found a gut-level freedom to do what they want to do. That is true freedom!

No, deciding to turn your will and life over to the care and direction of God does *not* mean you must shelve your brain, stifle your individuality, or sacrifice your lifelong desires. To do any one or all of these is to resign as a human being and this is not the intent here. By making this decision you are not *checking out* on humanity, you are *checking in*.

Blurred Vision

Most of the unhealthy dimensions of self-denial are produced by a blurry view of who God is. In general, the views of God fall into negative or ineffective categories such as an abusive father figure, a wimpy and frail Father Time figure, a Cosmic Killjoy, or a Hitler-type figure who employs an angelic gestapo to keep everyone in line. I understand how these and other blurry images have emerged over the years. However, the longer I live and the more I counsel those who are willing to take the risk of turning their wills and lives over to the care and direction of God as they understand Him, the more I am convinced that there is a loving God out there who uniquely and effectively responds to this kind of decision.

Not only have I seen this in others, but I know this to be true in my own personal experience as well. When I have come to this point of turning my will and life over to the care and direction of God as I understand Him, real and meaningful things happen for my good. God meets me right where I need to be met—at gut level!

I am not talking of spooky, weird, mystical things. I am talking about real and meaningful stuff!

Perspective I see myself differently. I see the problem differently. I see others in a different light. My problem seems so much lighter.

Presence   I am overcome with a sense of not being alone in my struggles. That is life-changing in and of itself. Gone is the ache of loneliness that seems to bring with it an intense panic or depression.

Power   I have a fresh, new confidence that I can get through whatever the problem happens to be at the time. This is accompanied by a rejuvenating strength to face the obstacles ahead.

Perspective, presence, and power are the most significant ingredients in creating the *hope* that I need to get through it all. Therefore, whatever the problem, I have the hope that I am not just going to make it through, but that I will be the better for it all as well! Now, that's what I call *real and meaningful stuff*. I know of no one who wouldn't want this kind of stuff!

How Do You Do It?

So, what does it mean to make a decision to turn your will and life over to the care and direction of God as you understand Him? How *do* you Look Up? How do you do it? In my experience, there are three vital ingredients that must be present. Each one is extremely difficult, and there simply is no easy way around it.

The first is that you must be *desperate!* You can't turn your will and life over to the care and direction of God until you face your own desperation. You may say this all sounds logical and makes so much sense, but that is not enough. Unless you come to your own desperation point concerning your problem, you will not be able to truly and completely turn over your will and life to anyone.

Some call this desperation point "hitting the wall" or "hitting bottom." Others call it "kissing concrete"! It's the point at which you are desperate enough to do something about your problem. You must come to the place in your life where you say, "OK, I realize there is no way that I can make this life work without God or someone greater than myself."

A few years ago my wife, Carol, and one of our neighbors were sitting on our back deck discussing the alcoholic scene in our community and what a good example the recovery world is to us. As our neighbor expressed how dedicated recovering alcoholics are about attending meetings and working on their problem, Carol said, "It's true. But you see in the case of alcoholics, they are *so* desperate!" They both agreed that the alcoholics have some kind of special problem. I couldn't help myself as I overheard their conversation. I opened the screen door and burst out saying, "But aren't we all that desperate, really? Aren't we all as desperate as the alcoholic or the drug addict?" My response was a surprise awakening for me! I came to realize through that interchange that I am *absolutely* that desperate. Until you face how desperate you really are, you cannot effectively turn your will and life over to the care and direction of God.

There are at least four desperation points. The first is a *tragedy or crisis in your life.* Many people finally sense their desperation at such a point. The loss of something or the loss of someone near and dear to you usually works.

Amazingly, though, too many people will take such a crisis in stride and move right through it. It seemingly doesn't even faze them! It's like they gut up for the next one and have to be knocked around again. Just how much are you prepared to lose?

The second is the exasperation of *repeated failures*. The desperation point here occurs when you become tired of repeated failure and continual screwups to the point of being worn-out. You become "sick and tired of being sick and tired." This brings on an emotional and physical exhaustion. How much can you take?

The third desperation point comes after the *wreckage of relationship after relationship*. It's when you are building up a pretty consistent track record of hurting the ones you love most. It comes when you take a look back over your shoulder at the path of destruction you have left behind you. It's the realization that all of the wreckage and the trashing of relationships isn't worth it. How many more people will you trash before you make your decision?

The fourth desperation point comes with the *fear of death and disease*. It's the fear of death and disease caused by any number of things—smoking? drinking? drugs? cancer? AIDS? stress? loneliness? heart attack? Are you dying a slow death brought on by your own problems in coping with life? What is it going to take for you to face how desperate you really are?

Recently, I heard a lecturer call the point at which you face your desperation a *conversion experience*. He was not referring to a religious experience, but a pivotal point of change in your life. It's a conversion in which you finally hear the wake-up call. Each of these desperation points is a wake-up call communicating to you that *enough is enough!* You must say to your problem, "Enough is enough! I'm not going any farther with this problem by myself. I need help in living my life! I'm going to turn my will and life over to the care and direction of God." You've got to be desperate enough to do it.

The second vital ingredient necessary for you to turn over your will and life to God is you must not try to make deals with God. "God, I'll tell You what I'll do, if You. . . ." This is not a time for deals. God doesn't make deals; He doesn't have to!

There is another way to make a deal of sorts. In a sense, either by hesitating or holding back you play the underdog, and the underdog usually gets his way just by waiting. It's attempting to force your way into the deal you wanted in the first place. This passive approach has reached almost epidemic proportions. People are *committed but not involved*. We do this on every front—we know what to do but simply don't do it. We are committed to our marriages, but not actively involved in them. We are committed to our children, but not actively involved with them. We are committed to our friends, but not actively involved with them. It's like the kamikaze pilot who made thirty-three missions—committed, but not involved!

Don't try to make a deal. Your deal has a built-in fizzle to it. When you turn your will and life over to the care and direction of God, it's on His terms, according to His agenda, and with His results. It's *His* deal, not yours. And it's the best deal you'll ever enter into!

The third vital ingredient needed for you to turn your will and life over to the care and direction of God is that you must *do it now*. You must be desperate enough, you can't deal with God, and you must do it now! Don't put it off. Don't wait. This decision is the next step you must take to turn your life around.

I realize that I am asking you to take a risk. But you are taking a greater risk by holding on to your problems and trying to handle them on your own. The risk I am asking you to take will be well worth it! *Life demands risks*. One anonymous writer put it this way:

To laugh is to risk appearing the fool. To weep is to risk appearing weak and sentimental. To reach out for another is to risk involvement. To expose your feelings is to risk exposing your true self. To place your ideas, your dreams, before the crowd is to risk their being lost. To love is to risk not being loved in return. To live is to risk dying. To hope is to risk despair and disappointment. To try is to risk failure and rejection. But, risks must be taken because the greatest hazard in life is to risk nothing. The person who risks nothing does nothing, has nothing, and is nothing. He may avoid suffering and sorrow, but he simply cannot learn, feel, change, grow, love and live. Chained by his certainties, he is a slave. He has forfeited freedom. Only a person who risks is truly free.

So, how do you do it? How do you turn your will and life over to the care and direction of God as you understand Him? Before I take you through that simple yet life-changing decision, let me show you how resigning as God will also enable you to reclaim your life!

4
Reclaim Your Life

Most people make a decision to turn their will and life over to the care and direction of God through the process of elimination—nothing else works. I especially like one anonymous statement that says, "Man occasionally stumbles over the truth, but most of the time he will pick himself up and continue on." This certainly has been true as people face the two decisions to Fess Up and Look Up. In fact, most would rather stumble around and keep going than actually face up to their problems and turn their lives over to any power other than themselves. The rewards for doing so are great. These rewards relate to more than just the immediate painful problems of life. They relate to life itself. It's tough for us humans to resign as God, but doing so places you on the road to reclaiming your life.

Let me demonstrate what I mean by the phrase *reclaim your life*.

Life: Like a Fleet of Ships

There is a wonderfully simple yet profound truth in the phrase, "Everything works best when it's plugged in!" The radio, the TV, the refrigerator, the toaster—all of these work only when they're plugged in. Human beings are no different. They work best when they are plugged in to their intended power source—God. When you actually turn your will and life over to Him you've found your source of power. You'll work better in every way—as a human being was meant to work. Then you can begin to reclaim your life. But what does it mean to reclaim your life? Simply to pull it all together and operate on all cylinders!

C. S. Lewis, the great Cambridge scholar and author, used an interesting illustration about a fleet of ships that explains it well. In a fleet of ships:

1. Each ship must be seaworthy.
2. The ships can't run into one another.
3. The ships must all be going in the same direction.

Using this image of a fleet of ships, I want to show you three benefits of plugging your life in to God and reclaiming your life in the process.

Each Ship Must Be Seaworthy

In a fleet of ships each ship must be seaworthy. In other words, if any or several or all of the ships in a fleet began to sink it would hardly be a normal and healthy fleet of ships. The same is true of human beings. Each individual must be "seaworthy." He must have an inward strength and stability that can be gained only through God.

Therefore, as we saw in chapter 3, the first benefit of turning your will and life over to God is personal *perspective:* inner perspective on your life—your identity, your relationships, and your responsibilities. This inner perspective has the potential to change your life. It's the ability to see all things differently—as possibilities rather than as problems. It's as if life consisted of pieces of a puzzle and God is the picture on the puzzle box. Without the picture on the box, the puzzle pieces are meaningless. That's the kind of perspective that is yours for turning yourself over to God! You become "seaworthy."

We all have the need for security and to know that we are able to float and not tip over or sink. This need is met with the kind of perspective that comes from turning our fragmented lives over to the care and direction of God. Without such perspective, we lose our direction and bearing and don't know where we've been, where we are, or where we're going. It's not that you have all of your problems solved, but you can see life, relationships, and your problems more clearly and more confidently. When your ship is seaworthy, you have a healthy perspective on how to maneuver your ship (your life) through the troubled waters that you are bound to face.

Ships Can't Run Into One Another

In a fleet of ships, the ships can't be running into one another. Can you imagine how ridiculous that would be? Each ship must be aware of the other ships that are in the fleet and be careful not to bump into any of them and create any damage. This is how it is in life as well. Each of us must be aware of the others around us and be careful not to bump into them in a damaging way.

This brings us to the second benefit of turning your will and life over to God—presence. When you turn your life over to the care and direction of God, not only is the invisible presence of God felt, but also the visible presence of God is seen through other people. You no longer have to face the struggles of life alone. People are no longer interruptions in your life. On the contrary, relationships with them become absolutely necessary. A great illustration of this comes from Woody Allen's film *Annie Hall*. At the end of the movie Woody Allen appears on the screen facing the camera and tells this corny old joke: "A man went in to see a psychiatrist. He said, 'My wife thinks she's a chicken.' He explained his wife's strange behavior to the doctor, and the doctor said, 'That's ridiculous! Why don't you tell her she's not a chicken?' The man immediately responded, 'Because I need the eggs!' " Isn't that the way it is? Relationships are difficult, irrational, and very painful sometimes, but you need what they give in order to survive in this world.

A great benefit of turning your life over to God is that you have a new sense of appreciation of the value of relationships. It's not that all your relationships will now run smoothly, but that you will fight for *their* survival rather than fight for *your* survival! This is because you know that if the relationship survives, you will survive much better and longer.

The benefit of presence through relationships is one of the great necessities for living life to the fullest. When you turn your life over to God, you see people in a new and fresh light. You become more open to what a true friend can really mean. Remember, a true friend is someone who leaves you with all of your freedom intact, yet obliges you to be *fully* what you are.

Ships Must Move in the Same Direction

A fleet of ships just wouldn't be a fleet of ships unless they all moved in the same direction. Each one has the same sense of destiny. Each one is heading toward the same goal. As a fleet they are pulling in unison toward that goal. People need the same kind of dynamic direction in order to be healthy. When you plug in to God, the third benefit is *power*. This power is the rejuvenating strength that moves you along into the future. It's the confidence that you can get through whatever the problem happens to be—the confidence to face it all. This power gives us the hope we need to go on.

The hope that I am talking about, however, is not a pie-in-the-sky hope or one filled with empty expectations or what I call the "it trap": If only I could live in that house with the beautiful view, that would be *it!* If only I could make that much money, that would be *it!* If only I could get married, that would be *it!* If only we could have children, that would be *it!* If only I could get divorced, that would be *it!* But when you get to *it*, inevitably somebody took *it.* It is never there, when you get there! The hope I *am* talking about simply says, whatever the future holds I can and will go on.

The benefits of turning your will and life over to the care and direction of God are for real. These benefits empower you to reclaim your life in order to live it to the fullest.

So why not do it—*now!*

How do you do it? How do you turn your will and life over to the care and direction of God as you understand Him? It's a matter of resigning as God and reclaiming your life. I have taken thousands of people through a simple prayer that has proven to be very effective. Don't put it off. Do it right now!

> Dear God, I really am desperate enough to make this decision. I don't want to make any deals with You, so right now, I want to resign as God of my life. I turn my will and life over to Your care and direction.

Part III
Clean Up!

Step #4   *Made a searching and fearless moral inventory of ourselves.*

Step #5   *Admitted to God, to ourselves, and to another human being the exact nature of our wrongs.*

5
Moral Surgery

In Part I the action-step was Fess Up; in Part II it was Look Up. Now, in Part III, it is Clean Up.

Clean up your act! Of all of the action-steps this is the one that is skipped over most easily. And in my experience this is the toughest step for people to move through. If you thought the first two action-steps were the most difficult, you're in for a real surprise.

It's not that people are prone to skip this action-step entirely, but the temptation is to apply it in a shallow manner. You see, this action-step of cleaning up your act requires surgery! And proper surgery means you have to cut deep enough to effect some real changes. The tendency is to cut only the surface, scream loudly about the pain, and act as though you have done the job. This approach, at best, is substituting the use of first aid for major surgery. It's like using a Band-Aid on a hemorrhage—easy to apply, but the patient is likely to die! No, what is des-

perately needed is major surgery—a searching and fearless moral inventory.

In this section I want to get behind the problem—the
biggie. I want to go underneath and identify the core of it.
There, we will discover the character defects behind the
problem—the whys. The core houses the nasty character
defects that are the root causes of the biggies and the
not-so-biggies we are continually fighting.

A few years ago I had one of the most depressing in-
sights I've ever faced. If I were able to take a magic wand
of some kind and wave it over this book empowering it to
solve your problems if you read it, it wouldn't help you
much at all. Not even if you carefully applied it. Why?
Because you would not have searched for the core of your
problems—the *reasons* behind the behavior. So, either the
same problem would return or another problem would
emerge to take its place. You would simply be swapping
one problem or addiction for another.

Problems and addictions are being traded back and forth
all the time. Years ago, a well-known singer made a dramatic move away from his drug-filled life-style into a new,
highly committed religious life-style. His conversion was
instantaneous. The secular world watched with a suspicious eye to see the outcome while the religious world
basked in this newfound victory—another sinner had seen
the light and returned to God! It was a royal welcome into
the spiritual ranks—for a few years.

As this singer made the rounds of the Christian concert
circuit, though, the "honeymoon" began to wear off. The
Christian crowds became very critical of his popular, secular songs and started to doubt his sincerity and commitment. After a while, he was picked up by the police on a
traffic violation, and in his car, they discovered a stash of
cocaine—his longtime drug of choice.

What was really happening? This well-meaning singer made the most common mistake made in the addictive world. His instant conversion and miraculous change only glossed over the core problems underneath his cocaine problem. In other words, he swapped his addiction to cocaine for a new addiction—an addiction to Christianity. Coke was out—God was in! But he did not deal with his core problems, the problems that led him to cocaine in the first place. When you merely swap addictions, you never really get over the original one.

This happens repeatedly with addictions and with problems in general! Alcoholics are famous for swapping their alcohol for tobacco. They trade one deadly chemical for another. Once they were "the drunks" and now they are "the chimneys"! And it is very common for the chemical addict to trade in his chemical for a variety of other addictive behaviors.

Often the new addiction is *cause* oriented. The workaholic gets his high from his work, therefore he places excessive focus on his job. The exercise nut finds his high through the discipline of exercising; the religious fanatic, in an all-consuming, heavenly focus upon the spiritual with a disregard for any and all forms of the material, earthly world around him. Each of these cause-oriented addicts is on a mission to prove something—to win people to his way of thinking and to avoid facing the reality of his own painful existence.

Trading addictions gets you nowhere closer to facing the real problems that are keeping you from enjoying your life to the fullest. This is because there are a few deadly core problems—character defects—ever-present, which provide a seedbed for all your problems to sprout and blossom into major trouble.

Examine Yourself

It's time to get on with the cleanup.

Step #4   *Made a searching and fearless moral inventory of ourselves.*

The first major phase in cleaning up your life is to examine yourself. This will take major surgery—a searching and fearless moral inventory. Moral surgery!

As I researched this area for the most basic issues, I was looking for some universal measuring sticks that are always true of the human condition. Although there are several sources that seemed right—the Ten Commandments, the Beatitudes, the Sermon on the Mount, and so on—none seemed quite right for getting to every core problem imaginable. Then, as I closely examined a very popular list, originally developed and taught by the Catholic church, I found what I believe to be the most helpful tools in performing this moral surgery. This list is known as the seven deadly sins:

Pride
Greed
Lust
Gluttony
Envy
Resentment
Laziness

Over the years I have discovered that inner-core problems have two things in common. The first is bad news: Each problem spells trouble for life. There is no way to permanently remove these deadlies from your life. They are part and parcel of the human condition. You can't get rid of them. The second is good news: Each of these dead-lies can be translated in life. The story doesn't end with the bad, depressing news; there is hope! You can use these deadlies to promote personal growth individually and re-lationally. In fact, if you don't learn to use them, they will most certainly *abuse* you.* Look for yourself in each of these "deadlies" as we examine them.

Deadly #1—Pride

Someone said, "Don't let your pride become inflated—you may have to swallow it someday!" Pride is probably the most popular of the deadlies. It also seems to be the easiest to confess as your own. We joke about it, laugh it off, and criticize it in others, but it is still prevalent and deadly to us personally. There seems to be little protection from its interference.

Pride can make a man forget his humanity and consider himself equal with God. It's a high-mindedness, a sense of superiority, and a vanity that looks down on almost ev-eryone else. Prideful people are blinded by their own im-portance. They view themselves as the primary reference point to life. Now, certainly there is a good side to pride—a self-respect we must all have as God's creations. But don't con yourself into thinking you have only the good pride without a trace of the bad—pride comes in all kinds of packages.

The Critic—This is a person who becomes defensive if he doesn't get his own way and reacts by shooting back when he feels shot at. He fails to see the other side of the issue and becomes intensely critical.

* A tape series, *The Seven Deadlies,* is available to assist you through Game Plan for Living, P. O. Box 316, Corona Del Mar, California 92625.

The Revenger—This type of prideful person is bent on taking revenge, getting back or getting even.

The Blamer—This is the person who is irresponsible for his own actions and feels the need to blame everyone and everything else when something goes wrong!

The Comparer—This person delights in comparing himself with others in order to be seen in a better light than the less-than-greats and seen as deserving of the spotlight equal to the greats.

The Controller—A controller must do it all himself. "No one can do it as well or as right as I can, so I'll have to do it myself!"

The Statue—Pride makes this type fearful of failure. He cannot or will not do something that makes him look foolish. He ends up doing very little!

The Proxy—This is a person who uses his children as pawns of pride. He wants his children to do certain things, be a certain way, look a certain way in order to impress the world that he's a good, even exceptional parent.

The Victim—This prideful person thinks he deserves more than he has received. "I'm just as good as that other person, so why does he have and I don't!"

The Fool—This person's pride is blatant—haughty, rude, manipulative, self-seeking, boastful, arrogant, lording it over others.

There are so many varieties of pride, it's impossible to list them all. But we are all guilty of this deadly sin to some degree. That's the bad news. Pride lurks inside all of us like a deadly toxin just waiting for an opportunity to express itself.

The good news? Pride can be translated in life. Translate pride into *humbling yourself before God*. Either humble yourself or you will be humbled.

Deadly #2—Greed

Psychology Today called the eighties the "Decade of Greed."[1] Greed causes you to aggressively take what you want by whatever means it takes to get it. It could be defined as covetousness—wanting things other people have. Basically, greed is selfishness—being stingy, keeping what you have for yourself only.

Greed may be seen in the miser—the person perpetually increasing for self, hoarding, and never letting go. But there are many other snapshots of greed in our world: the person who gets rich by cheating others . . . who takes advantage of the poor . . . who splurges to make himself feel better . . . who acts like a family vulture—always hovering to take his share *and* yours . . . who compromises personal standards to make the deal . . . who strives to keep up with the Joneses . . . who holds so tightly to what he has that he can't enjoy it.

Greed is everywhere! But as prevalent as greed is, it also can be translated. Translate greed into *personal contentment*. As soon as you recognize greed raising its ugly head, use it to appreciate what you already have and learn something about being content.

Deadly #3—Lust

I realize lust takes many different forms. There is a lust for power, a lust for recognition, and a lust for riches. But the lust I want to focus upon here is sexual lust. Lust is a distortion of sexuality, a runaway, uncontrolled sexual passion. It's a consuming desire for that which is wrong, a desire to use a person sexually for personal satisfaction.

There seem to be three levels of lust. First comes the thought level. At this level most people believe lust is under control and harmless, but this is equivalent to the match dropped in the dry forest.

The next level of lust is the acting out level. Thoughts turn into action. That which was only fantasy has now become reality.

The third level is addiction. It's at this level that your lust becomes a driving force—your thoughts are obsessed with it and you will do anything to fulfill your lustful desires—no matter the consequences!

The results of this deadly are extremely devastating. You become enslaved by your lust. You soon realize that your lust only leads away from a whole relationship and breeds loneliness, heartache, and disenchantment. Lust is risky business. Once you have identified how lust is at work inside you, then determine to grab hold of it in order to use it to your advantage. Translate lust into *personal purity and wholesomeness*.

Deadly #4—Gluttony

For some reason I have always considered gluttony to be the problem of eating too much and too often—sort of a worship of food. But as I examined it more closely I came to realize that it has to do with more than just eating. Gluttony is more accurately defined as loose living, pleasure seeking.

Gluttony has many facets. There's the Hugh Hefner philosophy of pure pleasure or doing whatever makes you feel good, which is principally focused on the self. The party animal who believes life is a party. The person who binges for comfort. The drinker who believes he can drown his problems. Gluttony could even include the shopper, the gambler, or anyone who is seeking pleasure in an obsessive manner, excluding other people and the rest of life. Gluttony acted out in this manner can become a life-style.

We all have a degree of gluttony within us, but gluttony can be used for personal growth. Translate your gluttony into *personal self-control.* I have found that if I am going to gain self-control in any amount, it comes through this channel most naturally.

Deadly #5—Envy

I've heard it said that when you feel yourself turning green with envy, you're ripe for trouble! Envy is that feeling of displeasure produced by witnessing or hearing of the advantage or prosperity of another person. Envy is that feeling of satisfaction or gladness when another person falls or fails.

Envy is both passive (in the mind) or active (acted out). Passive envy is found mostly in comparison—comparison of personality, looks, ability, popularity, position in life, and so on. Active envy is linked to several ugly companion problems. These companions, like gossip, criticism, undercutting, belittling, serve to mask the real problem of envy.

Envy is very insidious as it lurks around inside us. In the Wisdom Literature of the Bible we are warned that envy will always ultimately lead to disorder and every evil thing. Without a doubt, envy is one of the most destructive of all the deadlies. But envy, too, must be translated. Translate your envy into *personal trust in God.* Without this personal trust in the One who is more powerful than ourselves, I'm certain we could never win out over this deadly sin of envy.

Deadly #6—Resentment

Isn't it interesting that there is only one letter difference between the two words *danger* and *anger.* Anger may be the most misunderstood emotion in our world. It is not always as bad as most of us have been led to understand. In fact, anger, itself, is neutral, but when it is not expressed and festers, it turns into deadly resentment. Many believe that this deadly destroys more than any of the other seven.

Resentment can be seen in two kinds of people: The first is the *Exploder*. We all know about this person. He is obviously angry and has announced it by the explosion. Whether he is also storing and festering that anger is not readily known. The second is the *Imploder*. His anger is not so obvious. The exterior of the Imploder masks his anger with a nonexpressive look of almost calm. But the explosion is happening within! How a person expresses his anger is not as important as how the anger is being processed. It's the unprocessed anger that produces resentment.

There are as many types of resentment as there are people. It's usually accompanied by a negative attitude—pessimism about life to the point of depression. Resentful people are difficult to be around. Much of the time resentment paralyzes a person and makes him unable to take constructive action. Resentment gnaws away at your self-esteem and stunts your growth—personally and relationally. The trail of life is covered with the damaged relationships of the person filled with resentment. Studies continually demonstrate that the results of resentment are abusive and violent behavior, physical disease and psychological problems, and the constant state of dissatisfaction. For every minute of resentment you lose sixty seconds of happiness. Don't allow anger to fester and turn into resentment. Deal with it. Process it. Use it to promote your growth process. Translate resentment into *personal peace.* You see, resentment is your choice—choose it and fall to pieces; reject it and find peace.

Deadly #7—Laziness

The last deadly is crucial because you can't fight off the others without it. Laziness means not doing something you know you ought to do. It's being sluggish, dull, not energetic or vigorous, or moving very slowly so as to move with little or no pain or discomfort.

In my experience there are three types of lazy people: First, there are the *Regretters.* Regretters live in the past. They spend most of their time regretting either what happened or what didn't happen in the past. Since their focus is in the past, very little happens in the present. Second, there are the *Procrastinators*, who live in the future. Their theme song is "Tomorrow"—to the point that nothing gets done today! John Greenleaf Whittier's famous line is appropriate for this form of laziness: "For all sad words of tongue or pen, the saddest are these 'It might have been.' "

The third type of lazy people are the *Dreamers.* Dreamers are not necessarily stuck in the past or the future. They are suspended in the present. They would rather think about it than do it!

All of these types have one thing in common: They give up too soon. Some of the contributing factors to giving up are fear of failure, indecision, lack of direction, self-centeredness, and a desire to avoid pain. So, it's just simpler to take the easy way out—don't do anything.

Most of us workaholics hate to admit that we have any thread of laziness within us, but I think you can easily identify your own tendencies toward this deadly. When you recognize laziness to any degree, you can use it for

good. Translate your laziness into *perseverance*. Hang on to
laziness and you'll have an empty craving the rest of your
life. Persevere and you'll fill that craving.

Natural Response = Wrong Response

As you examine yourself in the mirror of these deadlies,
it's all too natural to respond in the wrong way. The first
response is to blame others for these problems in your life
or relationships. This reaction usually results in attempting to change the people around you.

The second response is to make excuses. You believe
you are the innocent victim of circumstances. Therefore,
you believe the answer is to attempt to change the conditions you face.

There is a very big flaw in these two strands of thinking:
Much of the time it is *impossible* to change either the people
or the conditions in your world. Therefore, you must come
face-to-face with the only thing you can change—*yourself.*
You must change yourself. You must Clean Up!

You Are Wanted in Surgery

If you are going to Clean Up, you must take this first
brutal step of moral surgery. You must examine yourself.
It's like taking a bath—no one can do it for you! Let me
make four simple suggestions as you begin your surgery:

1. Set aside a block of time—*alone!* Go away so
    that you are protected against interruptions.
2. Use pen and paper to record your findings.
    This in itself is a therapeutic exercise. Be sure
    to record your feelings in each of these cat-
    egories. Begin with "I feel . . ." and let it
    flow!

3. As you begin, pray for God's help. Listen for His guidance. He will help you get to your inner core and clean it out.

4. Search out all of the seven deadlies. Work through one deadly at a time. Write down where the deadly reveals itself: personally, relationally, and vocationally. You may not finish all seven at one sitting. But don't give up. Keep at it.

When you finally face yourself, you will find genuine relief.

6
Complete
Confession

A minister and a new convert were playing a round of golf together. As they teed off on the fourth hole the minister hit a respectable shot right up the fairway. The new convert squared off and sliced a horrible shot into the wooded area to the right of the fairway. He was *angry*. He pounded his club repeatedly against the ground, screaming, "I missed! I missed! I can't believe how badly I missed!"

This outburst of anger shocked the minister, but he decided to just ignore this childish scene from his newly converted friend. All went pretty well for the next two holes, but then the new convert lost it again on the seventh tee. Again he went berserk, but this time the minister couldn't hold back. He felt compelled to counsel this young man with respect to his crazy, irrational actions.

The minister asked, "Have you ever heard of Zapriel?" The new convert knew nothing of such a person. "Well, Zapriel is an angel whose total responsibility is to search the earth for those who become unusually angry over inconsequential things. And when he finds such a person, he will swiftly do his duty. Thunder will roll! The clouds will part! And all of a sudden Zapriel will thrust a ball of fire out of the sky down to the earth and will burn that person's body to a crisp. Now I'm warning you. Watch yourself. If you don't turn from your irrational ways, you are going to burn!''

The new convert was blown out with this story. He was sure that he had never signed on for this kind of thing. But he definitely got the minister's point—he had to control himself.

There was a small lake on the twelfth hole. In order to manage this hole most effectively it was best to shoot over this little body of water. The minister easily maneuvered over the lake and was all set up for his next shot. The new convert topped his ball, and it bounced directly into the water. His first reaction was to explode with anger, but he quickly remembered the minister's words and controlled himself. He decided to try another shot just to prove to himself that he could actually go over the water. He hit it wrong again, and again the ball went into the water. Without even hesitating, he teed up another ball and another and each of them went no farther than the bottom of the lake! Shaking with frustration he glanced up into the sky.

He pounded his club into the ground and yelled, "Oh, shucks! I missed!" He threw each of his clubs one by one into the lake. Then his hat, his shoes, his shirt, and finally his golf bag. As he stood there screaming "I missed!" over and over, thunder began to roll. The clouds parted and a ball of fire appeared in the sky. In an instant, the ball of fire shot out of the sky toward earth and burned the minister's body to a crisp! At this point you could hear only the sizzle from the fire and a strange voice out of the heavens screaming, "Oh, shucks! I missed!"

Zapriel *really* blew it. He missed his chance to fulfill his sole responsibility! If you miss out on Steps 4 and 5, you have really missed out on life!

In the last chapter, Step #4 of the Twelve Steps brought us to the point of performing major, moral surgery on ourselves—

Step #4   *Made a searching and fearless moral inventory of ourselves.*

The primary focus here was to examine yourself. Now we come to the second part of the Clean Up phase,

Step #5   *Admitted to God, to ourselves, and to another human being the exact nature of our wrongs.*

As you are coming out of surgery you must expose yourself.

Expose Yourself

The character defects—pride, greed, lust, gluttony, envy, resentment, and laziness—cannot be removed. We must find some other way to win the never-ending battle against them. Translating them into positive prods that will help us learn character qualities can be a tremendous help: pride into humility, greed into contentment, lust into personal purity and wholesomeness, gluttony into self-control, envy into trusting God, resentment into personal peace, laziness into perseverance. But there is something else that is very important in overcoming these seven deadlies. It's what I call complete confession.

Complete Confession

It is common knowledge that "confession is good for the soul." There is unusual healing in the midst of the dynamic of confession. I am not talking about simple confession, but *complete confession*. We really are as sick as our secrets. As long as we are able to "get by" without opening up about our inner defects we will do it. The old cover-up and hiding that has been going on since Adam and Eve tried to hide from God is prevalent within all of us. There is no way to overcome the seven deadlies without an effective confession and exposure of yourself.

There are three dimensions in a complete confession. The first is to confess to God. Now, God is the safest of all. He isn't going to tell another soul. He doesn't immediately talk back. He does not argue with me, and I am under a constant illusion that I can hide from Him when I need to do so. The second part is to confess to yourself. You're also quite safe. Even though you may confess to yourself, you still are able to use your mental and psychological powers of denial and rationalization. Therefore, confessing to myself is not necessarily a very big deal. The third dimension is to confess to another human being. This may be the toughest of all. In my opinion, this dimension of the complete confession is what makes confession the most powerful single dynamic any individual can exercise. It's just not easy to expose yourself in front of another person.

The early Christian church practiced confession as a regular part of their experience together when they assembled. As the church became more and more organized, confession within the church meetings was replaced by confession to a leader or priest. This was formalized within the Roman Catholic church for several centuries until the Reformation confronted this issue as well as many others.

But the Reformation never went far enough. This is especially true with respect to confession. Confession to a priest was replaced by encouraging the individual believer to confess directly to God. It was a liberating concept all right; it freed the church from the powerful dynamic of confessing to one another. The church or any other group of humans doesn't have a chance when the dynamic of confession is removed from normal experience.

There is a passage in the New Testament that states this principle in the simplest form: "Confess your sins to one another, and pray for one another, so that you may be healed . . ." (James 5:16). We are as sick as our secrets. But with the dynamic power of confession there is substantial healing.

How to Confess Completely

There are two ingredients that are necessary to confess completely. First, you need a person you can trust. A trustworthy person is vital. It can be a friend, a counselor, a minister, even a small group. And you will have to find this trustworthy person yourself. He's not going to look *you* up! If you can't readily identify such a person, then search for him through small-group involvement.

Second, you need to follow a process. You need a trustworthy person to listen to you as you tell the truth about yourself the best you can. The process is simple: Start out by saying, "I need your help!" Once you have made this or a similar statement the rest will begin to flow.

After one seminar session a young man approached me. Tense and fearful, he cautiously confessed that he had never been able to make love with his wife in their first seven years of marriage without thinking of another woman to whom he had been engaged. "I've never told a soul about this," he said. "What do you think I should do?" His secret produced heavy guilt. By telling me, he did the best thing he could have done—he confessed the exact nature of his problem to another human being. He was free! I've come to realize that in most cases this is 90 percent of the problem.

When you examine yourself, you face yourself and find *relief*. But when you expose yourself, you face another and find *release*. This is what I mean by Clean Up.

I saw an interesting label on a pair of pants: For best results—Machine wash, cold, separately—gentle cycle only. Do not bleach. Lay flat to dry. Warm iron. For not-so-good results—Drag behind car through puddles and blow dry on roof rack!

For best results—Clean Up, by examining yourself and by exposing yourself!

Part IV
Give Up!

Step #6 *Were entirely ready to have God remove all these defects of character.*

Step #7 *Humbly asked Him to remove our short-comings.*

7
Recycle Your Garbage

At this stage of moving through the Twelve Steps we have come to the fourth action-step—Give Up! In chapter 5, I urged you to perform major surgery. How well you performed this surgery will determine to a large extent how successful you will be at this next crucial action-step.

For all of us, there is a natural resistance to any kind of surgery: *Is it really necessary? I'm sure there must be some other way. Maybe if I just ignore it, it will go away.* Moral surgery is no different. It's not really necessary, you say, I'm not that bad off. I'll just "act" differently—that's all it will take, then people will see me differently and I'll see myself differently—no need to go any deeper. These two attempts at resistance are better known as *denial* and *rationalization*. And we're all good at them! But both, if applied, will nullify any attempt at successful surgery upon those character defects in your life—the seven deadlies.

If you were resistant to the action-step Clean Up, then you will be even more resistant to Give Up. Steps #6 and #7 are a natural follow-up to the major moral surgery:

> #6   *Were entirely ready to have God remove all these*
>   *defects of character.*
> #7   *Humbly asked Him to remove our shortcomings.*

If you don't want to perform the deep surgery, you will
certainly not be entirely ready for God to change you and
your life. It's one thing to admit your shortcomings to
God, but quite another to be ready to have Him remove
them. It's one thing to turn your will and life over to the
care and direction of God, but quite another to actually ask
Him to perform a cleansing work—inside out.

Shortcomings—Removed

The great hope in working through and applying the
Twelve Steps is the eventual removal of the problems that
are keeping you stuck in life. These are the problems you
identified in the Fess Up action-step at the beginning. The
lying, the fears, the drinking, the drugging, the guilt, the
sexual problems, the eating disorders, the anxieties—all
can be removed from their dominance in your life! The
dynamic of removal, however, does not mean that the
accompanying feelings surrounding the problem are mag-
ically removed as well. You may suffer a degree of loss in
these and other unlisted problem areas. The liar may lose
the attention he has gained by telling his thrilling stories
or may suffer loss when he faces the consequences of his
life-style of lies. The alcoholic loses the experience of taking that social or comforting drink. The drug abuser suffers the loss of his highs, which have bolstered him
through the struggles of life. All may lose certain
"friends," because of the pressure to act out in their problem area when they are around. Some may lose the priv-
ilege of going certain places because of the strong grip that

place has on them and their problem. Although you may suffer a degree of loss, you are experiencing in the present what it means to live your life on purpose and in a more meaningful way.

In other words, the dynamic of removal does not mean that your problem will never be a problem to you again. But it does mean that the more you are successful in working through these problems the stronger you'll become in your battle against them.

Seven Deadlies—Renovated

The seven deadlies are a different sort of problem altogether. These are not problems that lurk outside of you in the community, but they insidiously lurk inside you, awaiting their opportunities for destructive behavior. The seven deadlies are all part of the human condition. As they have become accustomed to expressing themselves through your personality, they are part of your own personal identity.

These are the problems behind the problems. After hundreds of hours of searching for the most basic problems of all, I have become convinced that there are no other root problems behind these: pride, greed, lust, gluttony, envy, resentment, and laziness. These are the primary culprits.

Three very common root problems mentioned by psychologists in today's popular self-help materials are fear, anxiety, and guilt. But these aren't core problems. In fact, they find their motivation and energy from the seven deadlies. They are most likely the three deadly symptoms that grow out of the seven core problems. But as deadly as these three are, they are still not as lethal as the continual presence of the seven deadlies.

The seven deadlies cannot be removed in the same way

you can remove the long list of other lesser problems. Instead of *removed*, I like the term *renovated*—changed for the better. It's almost like an exchange.

Exchange pride for humility, greed for giving, lust for loving, gluttony for responsibility, envy for rejoicing, resentment for love, laziness for work. Even though this work of renovation is not permanent, it helps you gain a degree of victory over the deadlies.

Failure—The Ticket to Healing

When you add all of this up, the conclusion is that the human condition isn't as totally wonderful as many propose. I like to say, there is a wonder about the human being, but there is a wickedness as well. The wickedness within all of us produces our failures. Probably the most dynamic message ever is this: In the midst of our failures— and only in the midst of our failures—there is power for personal renewal. Power is available for healing in the midst of our problems!

Teachings of Life

As you pay attention to the teachings of life around you, the principle that power is available for healing in the midst of our problems is quite clear, especially in times of death and dying. Over the years whether it is in the intensive care ward, at the bedside of one who is dying, or at a memorial service for one who has passed away, I've seen an amazing power displayed by human beings throughout these experiences. Some people immediately tap into this power. Others find it in the passing of time. Still others never seem to discover it at all.

Now, I'm not referring to a giddiness in the midst of tragedy. That's just another form of denial. The power I'm talking about is genuine. Those who find this incredible healing power have a peace that comes over them at their worst possible moment. It's a spiritual peace that sort of takes over. The possibility of death and dying triggers a clear wake-up call to most people.

With this in mind, it isn't any wonder college classes on "death and dying" are among the most popular on campus. Both Mitsuo Aoki at the University of Hawaii and Roger Blackwell at Ohio State University have enjoyed unusual success teaching on this subject year after year. When asked why they've had such phenomenal success, they are both quick to point out that what they are really teaching about is "life and living."

Teachings in the Jewish and Christian Traditions

The Messianic teachings within the Jewish Scriptures are filled with examples and lessons of the power that is available for healing in the midst of problems. There is repeated encouragement to cleanse your life, search your heart, repent in sackcloth and ashes, and confess your sins in order to receive the blessing of God. The entire ministry and teachings of Jesus continually emphasized the fact that God was searching to heal only those who admitted their need for God's Great Physician.

Teaching of the Grace of God

All of these teachings point to the most powerful and possibly most misunderstood principle ever taught—*the grace of God.* The foundation of the Twelve Steps is this grace of the Higher Power. It's the grace of God that enables Him to respond to our confessions and to willingly remove all our shortcomings—to offer healing to any and all of us, no matter who we are or what we've done. You see, grace is defined as "unmerited favor" from God Himself. It's undeserved. Not only are you unable to do anything to deserve it, you *couldn't* do anything if you tried!

Healing Grace

So, God freely offers His grace (unmerited, undeserved favor) to everyone. This grace produces healing for whatever the need and motivates us to choose good over evil and life over death and destruction.

Now, this isn't one of those religious terms—an empty God-word without meaning. It's a very real and tangible dynamic that must be put to the test. Grace must be applied. *Applied grace is healing grace.*

Healing grace allows you to take all that has happened to you and use it for good. All that has happened (all the garbage)—what you have done and what others have done to you—is designed for recycling. This is both to benefit you and for you to benefit others. God specializes in problems and difficulties. He works best in human crises, intensive care wards, and the cemeteries of our lives.

The results are absolutely incredible! Healing grace counters the gnawing guilt with genuine forgiveness . . . the bondage of fear with a boost of freedom . . . and the pain of anxiety with the presence of peace.

God wants to recycle your garbage in His Healing Grace. But you must ask Him to do so.

The healing grace of God is only as powerful as your Higher Power!

8
How High Is Your Higher Power?

We come now to the most sensitive section in this book. It's sensitive because of the subject matter presented. I know that who people identify as their Higher Power varies dramatically. And I also know that no matter how the Higher Power is identified, there have been phenomenal results by working through the Twelve Step program. You see, I'm convinced that most people's Higher Power is not high enough to actually remove the shortcomings as it says in Step #7. Therefore, in this chapter I am offering for your consideration only One whom I believe to be the most adequate Higher Power in existence. His name is Jesus.

Now, don't write me off quite yet. I realize that there are all kinds of religions and philosophical systems in our world—agnosticism, mysticism, atheism, pantheism, humanism, Zen Buddhism, existentialism. With people swinging from one side of the pendulum to the other, the result is that many are suffering from "ism-itis." "Ism-itis" is a sort of motion sickness caused from swinging on the pendulum or watching others swing. Because of the resulting dizziness, very few people have stopped long enough to consider the overwhelming evidence that the personal God of the universe has revealed Himself by written form (the Bible) and human form (Jesus of Nazareth) and desires a personal relationship with people. This is why I'm asking you to take the time in this part of the book to investigate this alternative as your Higher Power. I'm not asking you to buy it, just consider it.

The Supernatural Factor

I'm not talking about religion. Religion destroys people. Jesus told the religious leaders of His day that they were "snakes" and "painted tombstones." He was down on religion, and so am I. Years ago, when I wanted to obtain my "ticket to heaven," religion told me that there were fifteen things I couldn't do. As I looked over the list, immediate depression set in. Many of those things were my goals in life! Then I was told there were four things I could do—that I *must* do:

1. Go to church on Sunday morning
2. Go to church on Sunday evening
3. Go to church on Wednesday evening
4. Pray before every meal

It all spelled out a four-letter word to me—*BORE!* Then I ran into a group that said all I had to do to get my ticket was to let them dunk me in their tank. (This comes in various forms: sprinkling, squirting, drowning, dry-cleaning, etc.) The only thing I gained from that experience was a wet body. No, I'm not talking about religion.

Because it blindly accepts a certain system of do's and don'ts and ignores more basic issues, religion makes life miserable. It's comparable to a sedative given to a dying person. It may make him feel better, but he's still dying!

In my own spiritual search to know God, I finally came to understand that there is a *supernatural factor* in our world that I was forced to examine. As I worked through the evidence for this supernatural factor, I discovered that God is knowable and you don't have to shelve your brain to approach Him.

The supernatural factor is not a blind or mystical leap in the dark whereby one hopes to find meaning to life. It's based on evidence and logic. It's not one nebulous, evasive, or untouchable factor. Rather, it's a body of solid facts clearly laid out, upon which we can hang our faith.

To many people evidence means absolutely nothing. An interesting illustration of this is the old story of a man who thought he was dead. His concerned wife and friends sent him to the friendly neighborhood psychiatrist. The psychiatrist determined to cure him by convincing him of one fact that contradicted his belief that he was dead: the simple truth that dead men do not bleed. He put the patient to work reading medical texts, observing autopsies, and so on. After weeks of effort, the patient finally said, "All right, all right, you've convinced me. Dead men do not bleed." Whereupon the psychiatrist stuck him in the arm with a needle and the blood began to flow. The man looked down with a contorted, ashen face and cried, "Good Lord! Dead men bleed after all!"

If however, you *are* willing to consider the available evidence, examine it honestly, and make a reasoned evaluation, we can begin to think through the supernatural factor.

The Supernatural Revelation

First, consider whether the Bible, comprised of the Old Testament and the New Testament, is a revelation from God. In order for you to think this through, I'd like to offer you just a few reasons why I believe it is.

Unity

The first reason I believe the Bible is a supernatural revelation from God is that it has incredible *unity*. It was written over a period of fifteen hundred years, by forty different writers, in three different languages, and on three different continents. A lot of people think that some group back in Jerusalem—the First Bapterian Church of the Epistolics—got together and decided to write a bunch of books. Then year after year they submitted them to the University of Jerusalem, who at last one day put them to press and called them the Bible. That's simply not true! It was written over many centuries and yet with unbelievable unity. You can read modern books on different subjects, even from one university, from one school of thought, and you will find vast differences. There may be people working on the same committee, trying to come up with some sort of book, and they'll even disagree on what chapters should be included. So when you find a book written over a long period of time, in a number of languages, by people with wide cultural differences, and you still see unity—you have something worth considering. It's not a normal book!

Accuracy

The second reason I believe that the Bible is a revelation from God is its *accuracy*—archaeological accuracy and historical accuracy. I'm just going to give you a taste of each of these and try to highlight some of the evidence they offer.

Archaeological accuracy   I have enjoyed reading archaeology over the years, especially the works of Dr. Albright, professor emeritus at Johns Hopkins University. Dr. Albright was a brilliant scholar in his field, but when he moved out of archaeology into prophecy, the brilliance faded a bit. He made statements such as, "We can't find the Hittites!" (The Hittites were a large, much talked about group of people in the Old Testament.) Albright and his companions felt that if we could not find the Hittites, the Bible must be inaccurate. Then another archaeologist came along and discovered the Hittites! The most embarrassing moment in the life of an archaeologist turned prophet is when someone digs up what he said didn't exist. (By the way, Albright "prophesied" in 1948 that the Jews would not go back into their land and make it a state.) Nevertheless, Albright was a great archaeologist, and after a life of study and excavation in the Middle East, he concluded, "There can be no doubt that archaeology has confirmed the substantial historicity of Old Testament tradition."[1]

Albright's conclusion is supported by that of Sir Frederic Kenyon, the former director of the British Museum.

> It is therefore legitimate to say that, in respect to that part of the Old Testament against which the disintegrating criticism of the last half of the nineteenth century was chiefly directed, the evidence of archaeology has been to reestablish its authority and likewise to augment its value by rendering it more intelligible through a fuller knowledge of its background and setting. Archaeology has not yet said its last word, but the

results already achieved confirm what faith would suggest—that the Bible can do nothing but gain from an increase in knowledge.[2]

These experts attest to the Bible's archaeological accuracy!

Historical accuracy   There was a man by the name of Sir William Ramsay who set out to prove the Bible false by proving its historical events false, especially those in the Book of Acts. He decided he was going to go everywhere and do everything that Luke had recorded himself, Paul, and the others doing in the Book of Acts. His intent was to prove it couldn't be done. For example, taking a boat from one point to another in a certain period of time. He took the same kind of boat that they must have taken, left from the same place, and journeyed to the same place, trying to see if they could have made it in the recorded period of time. When he finished with his study, he concluded that Luke was probably the most accurate historian of his time.

> Luke is a historian of the first rank; not merely are his statements of fact trustworthy; he is possessed of the true historic sense; he fixed his mind on the idea and plan that rules in the evolution of history, and proportions the scale of his treatment to the importance of each incident. . . . In short, this author should be placed along with the very greatest of historians.[3]

He was overwhelmed with the Bible's historical accuracy!

Now this accuracy doesn't prove that the Bible is supernatural, but it does indicate that it is accurate in the details. And if it is accurate in the things that don't matter a whole lot, it stands to reason that it is more likely to be accurate in the things that do matter.

I think it is also important to point out how the biblical documents compare with other ancient documents. Tacitus was a Roman historian of the late first and early second centuries. One thousand years later, there were twenty copies of what he wrote. The original had been lost—only twenty copies existed. Caesar's *Gallic Wars* has the same kind of spread; only eight copies exist today. Thucydides, a Greek writer often cited, is represented by five or six documents after a period of thirteen hundred years.

No one is getting really upset about the accuracy of what these writers said. No one is very interested in it, and no one questions it. As Kenyon comments,

> Scholars are satisfied that they possess substantially the true test of the principal Greek and Roman writers whose works have come down to us, of Sophocles, of Thucydides, of Cicero, of Virgil; yet our knowledge of their writings depends on a mere handful of manuscripts, whereas the manuscripts of the New Testament are counted by hundreds and even thousands.[4]

When we bring the Bible into focus here and compare it with these other ancient documents, we find it is supported by the strongest evidence possible. Kenyon continues:

> It cannot be too strongly asserted that in substance the test of the Bible is certain. Especially is this the case with the New Testament. The number of manuscripts of the New Testament, of early translations from it and quotations from it

in the oldest writers of the Church, is so large
that it is practically certain that the true reading
of every doubtful passage is preserved in some
one or other of these ancient authorities. This
can be said of no other ancient book in the
world.[5]

There are thousands of manuscripts of portions of the
Bible, some of them written within sixty, fifty, and even
forty years of the event.

In the Old Testament we have a manuscript that is dated
A.D. 900. Because that used to be the oldest manuscript of
the Old Testament, many have speculated, "If the Old
Testament we have is dated A.D. 900, certainly a lot of
inaccuracies must have developed in the hundreds of
years before, a lot of bad copying and that kind of thing."
This kind of speculation leads to some very interesting
arguments. As a matter of fact, some Jewish scholars have
said that Isaiah 53 (which prophesies that the Messiah will
come and suffer for the sins of the world) was written by
the Church. "There's no doubt about it, it had to be; it
sounds too much like Jesus," they argue.

In Micah 5:2, it says that the Messiah will be born in
Bethlehem. Liberal scholars have estimated that Micah
was written about 250 B.C., but they are quick to make an
exception for that one verse. They don't like that verse,
because it talks about the Messiah being born in Bethlehem. That's supernatural! Therefore, it must have been
inserted after the event.

Then the Dead Sea Scrolls were found. These Old Testament manuscripts are dated approximately 150 B.C. All
of these scrolls (and they are still being worked on) have
proved to be 98.33 percent exactly the same as documents
dated later.[6] "It is a matter of wonder that through some-

thing like a thousand years the text underwent so little alteration." There were very few inaccuracies. Very few changes—it's amazing! Every book in the Old Testament is represented in the discovery of the Dead Sea Scrolls except the Book of Esther.

Isaiah 53 is there, and if you can read the Hebrew, you can go to the Shrine of the Scroll in Jerusalem someday and say, "Yes, that's it, that's Isaiah 53. I saw it!" It was not written by the Church, but was in existence for at least two centuries before the Church was founded.

> Of the 166 words in Isaiah 53, there are only seventeen letters in question. Ten of these letters are simply a matter of spelling, which does not affect the sense. Four more letters are minor stylistic changes, such as conjunctions. The remaining three letters comprise the word "light," which is added in verse 11, and does not affect the meaning greatly. . . . Thus, in one chapter of 166 words, there is only one word (three letters) in question after a thousand years of transmission—and this word does not significantly change the meaning of the passage.[7]

Micah 5:2 was there, too. All the things that had been thrown up as inaccuracies were there, a thousand years before the A.D. 900 manuscript.

I have a friend whose name is Arnold Fruchtenbaum. He's a Hebrew-Christian. Arnold's grandfather was the rabbi of the largest Hasidic (very conservative) Jewish sect in the world, located in Siberia, where he was born. His grandfather knew the Torah (the first five books of the Bible) so well that when a spike was driven through it, he could tell exactly which words it had touched on every page. That's an example of the standard of accuracy with which they copied and transferred the Word of God. They considered it the holy Word of God. They counted the words within the Book to make sure they had the exact number, and so many words on each page. They were very careful, and they produced a very accurate copy of the original.

Prophecy

In my opinion, a lot of bad press, most of which isn't worth looking into, has come out on prophecy. For instance, some have said that the red dragon in Revelation must mean China. Why is that? You can't reason from what you see around you and then decide what you want a verse to be talking about. When you are trying to find out what a verse in the Bible means, you have to study how it was used within its cultural setting. Some teachers of prophecy say that when Revelation speaks of people mounting up with wings as eagles and fleeing to the mountains it means that Israelis are going to be fleeing their land in United States airplanes (the eagle being a symbol for the United States). That's ridiculous! Such thinking has no controls. Whatever you think is there is there, and that's foolishness.

There are two prophecies that I believe can be clearly documented—Christ's first coming and Christ's second coming. In discussing the first coming I will mention nine specific prophecies that are very simple, but very interesting. When Christ came on the scene, there were two concepts concerning the Messiah: One was that the Messiah was going to come and reign, the other was that the Messiah was going to come and die. Now, if you were a Jew, sitting in captivity under the persecution and harassment of the Romans, which Messiah would you like to have come? It was not time for one to die, that's for sure! Although some were still holding to the two-Messiah concept at Christ's coming, there were many who believed just what the Old Testament prophesied. It said:

1. He would be born in Bethlehem.[8]
2. He would be preceded by a messenger.[9]
3. He would enter Jerusalem on a donkey.[10]
4. He would be betrayed by a friend.[11]
5. He would be sold for thirty pieces of silver.[12]
6. This money would be thrown down in God's house andgivenforapotters'field.[13]
7. He would not retaliate against His accusers.[14]
8. His hands and feet would be pierced.[15]
9. He would be crucified with thieves.[16]

Peter Stoner, in a book entitled *Science Speaks*, calculates that the possibility of a person fulfilling all nine of these would be one times ten to the seventeenth power. I'm not much of a mathematician, but I believe that's one with seventeen zeros following it, and those are high odds. Stoner made this analogy: Take that many silver dollars, one times ten to the seventeenth power, lay them on the surface of Texas, and they will cover all of the state two-feet deep; mark one of them, stir it up with the others, blindfold a man, and ask him to pick up the marked coin in his first try. One times ten to the seventeenth power. That's very difficult!

Now, if the number of prophecies were increased from nine to forty-eight (there are sixty major ones in all), consider the possibility of one person fulfilling all of them. These prophecies don't deal with generalities—such as it will be a depressing day, the economy will have a bad time, there will be clouds this month. They are very specific. The possibility that all forty-eight of these would by chance be true of one man is one times ten to the 157th power. That's a lot of zeros![17]

One of the prophecies of Christ's first coming that is especially outstanding is Daniel 9:24–27. It says that 483 years after the decree to rebuild Jerusalem and its walls (given in 445 B.C.) the Messiah, the Prince, will come. I believe that's why many people, as we see in the Gospels, were looking for the Messiah at that time, because it was around A.D. 30 that He was to come.[18] That's a pretty accurate prophecy written 500 years before Jesus ever came on the scene.

The second coming is also very interesting. The Bible prophesies about what context the Messiah will come in and what state the world is going to be in when He comes to set up His Kingdom. In Leviticus 26, Deuteronomy 28, and Deuteronomy 30 we read that although Israel will be scattered throughout the world, she will return to her land and become a nation. The fulfillment of this occurred in 1949. It was also prophesied that she will take over the city of Jerusalem. This didn't happen until 1967, in the Six-Day War.

The third thing it says about Israel is that she will rebuild the Temple before Jesus comes back to reign. On the sixth day of the Six-Day War, when Israel was going in to take the city of Jerusalem, some scrolls were found at the edge of the city. These were called the "Temple Scrolls," and they were written up in *Time*, *Newsweek*, and other publications. The scrolls will be used as instructions to rebuild the Temple on its historic site.

As some of you know, this might present a little problem. You can't build a temple on the site until the little building presently there is moved off, and the little building presently on the site belongs to the Arabs. The Mosque of Omar (The Dome of the Rock) is the second most holy spot in the Islamic religion. One surefire way to get a few Arabs hot is to start knocking down that building! When Hildad, the Israeli historian, was asked, "When are you going to build the temple?" he said, "Well, it will probably take us a generation, just as it did with David when he came back from the land." They replied, "But what about that temple over there, what about the mosque?" He smiled and answered, "Maybe there will be an earthquake, who knows?" Jews who take the Old Testament seriously are talking about the Temple. They are even selling temple bonds, if you care to buy them, in Los Angeles or Miami.

There is also a prophecy in Ezekiel 38:1–9 which states that the King of the North (from the northernmost parts of Israel) will come and set up an alignment of powers with the nations immediately bordering Israel. If you take a line directly north from Israel, you come to the King of the North, which I believe is the Russian government. Whether they will be in the form they are now or not, I don't know. Neither do I know when all this will happen. I'm just trying to help set a possible context here. The Russian people did not go against Israel in an alignment of power with the Arab nations until 1967. They were trying to get Israel without going to war against her, so they armed the Arabs and took the side of the Arab people. It happened just as Ezekiel said it would.

It's also interesting to note that prophecy indicates the economic center of the world will be moved to the Middle East. In Zechariah 5:5–11 it says that the *ephah*, a Hebrew term used for the commercial center, will be moved to Shinar. Shinar is in the Middle East, and this prophecy indicates that before the Messiah comes back the economic center, the commercial center of the world, will be in Shinar. Who would have thought a few years ago that this Middle East oil mess would so radically alter world economics right now, in this time, in our day? Things seem to be falling into place for the Messiah to come back. I don't think it's wise to talk about time, but I do think it's interesting to see that world events are occurring just as the Bible said they would.

The ecological problems we are facing today are also talked about in the Bible. A lot of people say, "Hey, wait a minute, you can't talk about wars and rumors of wars and famines and earthquakes as being a fulfillment of prophecy. There have always been wars and rumors of wars; there have always been earthquakes!" That's true, but when Christ talks about these He speaks of them as birth pangs, and He says that there will be more and more of them, and they will be more intense. It's like the intensity of pain a woman experiences while giving birth to a child. The birth pangs occur more frequently and become more intense until finally she gives birth. That's the image that Christ is trying to present—unity, accuracy, prophecy—both of the first and of the second coming.

Claims of Christ

The fourth reason I believe the Bible is a supernatural revelation from God is the *claim to deity* that Jesus made. He came saying, "I am the God-Man." He said it in many ways:

> "If you've heard Me, you've heard God."[19]
> "If you've seen Me, you've seen God."[20]

"If you know Me, you know God."[21]
"If you've received Me, you've received God."[22]
"If you've honored Me, you've honored God."[23]

He was trying to get a point across—He was claiming to be equal to God. The chief priest walked up to Him in John 8 and said, "Are you the One who claims to be the Messiah, from the Old Testament?" and He said, "Yes, that's Me." Many liberal scholars would say He didn't mean that. He meant something "deeper." It's as if I were to see an old acquaintance and say, "Rob, are you the same Rob Wilson I remember attending the men's seminar a few years ago?" And he said, "Yeah, that's me." And I said, "Ah, really, you don't mean that, do you? You mean something 'deeper.' " No! He meant what he said—he's Rob Wilson. Jesus said exactly what He meant when He said He was the Messiah. A man who can read the New Testament and not see that Christ claims to be more than a man, can look all over the sky at high noon on a cloudless day and not see the sun.[24]

C. S. Lewis, one of the greatest scholars of our century, argues it this way: The claim of Jesus that He was the God-Man is either true or false. If it's true, Jesus is the God-Man. If it's false, either He knew it was false, or He didn't know it was false. If He knew it was false—He really knew He wasn't the God-Man, but He was running around anyway, saying, "I am the God-Man," what was He doing? Lying—He was an imposter! On the other hand, if He didn't know it was false—He thought He was the God-Man, but really wasn't—and He was running around saying, "I am the God-Man," what was He? He was nuts! That's it; those are the only alternatives we have. He was either lying, He was mentally unbalanced, or He actually was the God-Man.[25]

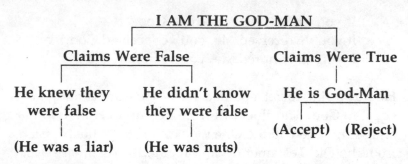

Some people try to draw a line right down the center of this and say, "He was an outstanding teacher, the most exemplary person in the history of mankind. In fact, He would have made 'Who's Who in Jerusalem' if He had stuck around long enough. Too bad He died." But wait a minute, He didn't leave that alternative open to us. Either He was a liar, or He was mentally unbalanced, or He was the God-Man. Period.

Passing Jesus off as an outstanding teacher or a great example after hearing His claims would be like passing me off as a "great guy" after hearing me claim I was a poached egg. Imagine for a moment that I am not Tim Timmons, and I tell you, "Hey, I'm not Tim Timmons, I'm a poached egg." (Some of you may think, *Um, could be.*) Now you would have to take me through the same kind of grid. I am either lying, mentally unbalanced, or I really am, I truly am, the first poached egg you have ever seen walk or talk. I guarantee though, after a very short time of my telling you that I am a poached egg, you would not say, "You know, even though he claims to be a poached egg, he's a great guy." You don't do that with people like that. You get help for them!

Napoleon Bonaparte said,

> I know men and I tell you that Jesus Christ is no
> mere man. Between Him and every other person

in the world there is no possible term of comparison. Alexander, Caesar, Charlemagne and I have founded empires. But on what did we rest the creations of our genius? Upon force. Jesus Christ founded His empire upon love; and at this hour millions of men would die for Him.[26]

Jesus claimed to be the God-Man and that claim is the best indication, the greatest proof, that there is something unusual about the Bible. He claimed that He was speaking from the Bible and that what He was saying was authoritatively coming from God. Many have claimed to be prophets or messengers *from* God. Jesus of Nazareth claimed to *be* God. He is the only man who has ever come along saying that He was the God-Man, and every one of us has to decide what to do with His claims.

So What?

There are basically four possible responses to this consideration of Jesus being the most adequate Higher Power.

1. Your Higher Power is in place, but you have not identified it with Jesus and you are satisfied with what you have. If this is your situation, I urge you simply to keep an open mind as you continue your spiritual journey.
2. Your Higher Power is in place, but is unidentified at this time. You're not sure that you are ready for Jesus right now. Keep searching and seeking to relate to the Higher Power.
3. Your Higher Power is in place, but unidentified at this time. This reasoning about Jesus

being the Higher Power makes sense to you
and you would like to pursue it. Read on.

4.   Your Higher Power is in place and you have
identified it as Jesus, but you have not experienced the Healing Grace explained in the
last chapter. Read on and see if you can find
some sort of clarification as to the dynamics
of a personal relationship with God.

The Supernatural Relationship

"The heart cannot enjoy what the mind cannot accept."
Because people continually ignore that principle, many
have emotionally accepted or rejected Christianity without
really understanding it. The biblical revelation is not just
another book of pious platitudes and religious rhetoric.
It's a supernatural revelation that explains life as it is and
people as they are. Built upon this crucial foundation is
the reality of the supernatural relationship.

The Plan

Everything works best when it's plugged in. Man is
certainly no exception to this. Man works best when he's
plugged in to God and His principles for living. But the
caricatures of God and His relationship with man run the
full spectrum from a mysterious Genie to an angry Tyrant.
Therefore, God's image and His principles are continually
blurred so that man doesn't know why, how, or where to
plug in!

Because of the blurriness, most people come into a personal relationship with God through the process of
elimination—nothing else works! But no matter how much
a person approaches God there is a definite universal plan

by which man can personally relate to God and His principles.

God's plan was to create man to be an active force against evil primarily by

reflecting God's image
reproducing godly children
reigning together over the earth (Genesis 1)

All of this was to be a positive force for God and against evil. As long as man remains plugged in to God and His principles, he will experience a more meaningful life-style (not trouble-free, but meaningful and fulfilled).

So if God planned such a life-style for man, then why is it not working for most people?

The Problem

The plan was beautiful, but man botched it royally. As the bumper sticker says, "If you feel far from God, who moved?" The problem? Man moved!

Original man, through the freedom that is inherent within humanity, chose to become unplugged from God. When offered the alternate life-style of living independent from God (even the possibility of equality with God), original man and woman bought in to it!

They chose to live life separated from God, and everyone since original man continually makes the same choice. It's a matter of options—me or God—and since the world must revolve around me, God loses out. "God, You go Your way; I'll go mine. Check with me when I'm seventy-one or seventy-two and we'll negotiate then." (Or sooner, if there's a major crisis!)

Man's choice to remain unplugged separates him from a meaningful life with God. The consequences of this separation from God are devastating. It's not just a spiritual separation from God, but also a psychological separation from man's true, healthy self and a social separation from other human relationships. Therefore, man (unplugged) suffers from one of the most penetrating problems of all— loneliness—feeling alienated from God, self, and others.

The gnawing pains of loneliness are a setup for any and every man-made scheme offering to help man escalate beyond himself to God or "God-likeness." The pain is so great, man is ready to try anything that will provide some sort of temporary, fast, pain relief! (A self-help book, a tape, a seminar, a drug, a drink, another person, a different location, a new toy, or a religious experience.) But no matter how much man crams into his life, nothing seems to satisfy him long-term. Why? Because man is unplugged. **Everything works best when it's plugged in!**

We have a desperate problem. We are separated from the God of the universe by our rebellion—the Bible calls it sin. It's like being separated by a great canyon that no one is able to cross on his own, even though we make many admirable attempts. Some try living a good life. Some give to charities. Many become religious. Others try the intellectual route. Still, no one is able to cross the canyon to the other side. It's humanly impossible!

Let's suppose that you and I are walking along the edge of a forty-foot canyon, and we want to get across to the other side. You suggest, "Let's jump!" I say, "All right, but you go first!" So you back up about fifty yards and run like crazy toward the edge. As you spring from your side you push off with every ounce of strength you can muster. It's a noble jump—thirty-five feet, eleven inches. When I see you jump, I back up about ten yards and run toward the edge, giving it all I've got—ten feet, five and one-half inches. As you are soaring through the air in front of me, you glance back and think how much better you're doing than I. However, in a few seconds, we are both lying at the bottom of the canyon in critical condition. Why? People can't jump forty-foot canyons—they need a bridge.

So God has a plan whereby man can live life to its fullest, but man continually rejects it. Instead of accepting God's plan, man tries to create the "ultimate" life-style all by himself. But in the process man creates his own self-destruction. This is man's problem. It is also God's dilemma, but He will not force Himself or His life-style upon anyone. Instead, God offers every man everywhere a way back into a personal relationship with Him.

The Payment

To put man's problem another way, he is in debt to God. For our self-centered rebellion (our sin), God requires a payment. One of the most natural instincts of man is to try to pay for his own guilt. Man feels he must pay for what he does wrong and for his shortcomings. Everyone attempts to pay in different ways. Some pay by being down on themselves, even to the point of depression. Others pay by depriving themselves of something. An increasing number are attempting to make the ultimate payment by killing themselves, but none of these self-imposed payments really satisfies. The debt remains—man is guilty before God.

Counseling rooms are filled with people who are guilt-ridden, seeking a payment that will give them the confidence that the debt is paid. Professional counselors offer three possible payments. First is the transfer method:

Blame it on the environment, blame it on society—"It's a wonder that anyone comes out healthy, living in such a sick society." Or blame it on your parents or your mate. Whatever you do, transfer the blame away from yourself. This will relieve your sense of responsibility in the situation so that you cannot be held responsible. It's true that we are all greatly affected by other people and circumstances, but a person must accept responsibility for his own actions. If he doesn't, who will?

The second method of dealing with guilt is to lower or do away with the standard or principle that was broken. "Who makes up these rules anyway?" If a person breaks the marital bond through an extramarital affair, then let's lighten the importance of the marital bond. Take this approach to its logical end, and you create a society in which everyone does whatever he decides is right. It seems this is one of the most popular themes today—"Do your own thing." (Sometimes known as, "If it feels good, do it!") The progression in this kind of reasoning is:

1. It all depends on how you look at it,
2. It really doesn't matter how you look at it, and finally,
3. I don't think anybody knows how to look at it.

Therefore, do your own thing. The result—chaos!

The third method used to deal with guilt is escape. Where? How about central Africa? Escape—to anyplace where you are unknown and cannot be pressured or reminded of your particular crisis situation. Without a doubt, "getting away" for a time may be helpful. But you cannot continue to run. In order to be freed from the guilt connected with a particular problem, you must face it head-on. Otherwise, it will never go away; it will hide in your subconscious waiting to haunt you.

All three methods of dealing with personal guilt are not really payments of the debt at all. They are simply methods by which we ignore the problem, hoping to alleviate the "guilts." Some people find temporary relief this way, only to despair later as the cancerous beast once again raises its ugly head. Many walk away from the counseling room in despair, because they are still weighted down with the guilt and have been given no hope or relief.

The only payment that works is the one that God Himself set in motion. Immediately after man rejected God's plan for living, God promised a "Deliverer," a "Messiah"—a way of plugging back in to God. This promise became the foundation for God's progressive deals with man throughout history. God made deals with man through Abraham, Moses, and David, and reconfirmed them through several Jewish prophets over the centuries.

Each of God's deals with mankind has been building upon the same underlying theme—a Deliverer is coming. This Deliverer will be from the family of Abraham, will personally fulfill the Mosaic Law, will be out of the nation of Israel, and, as a Son of David, will someday rule forever. All of these covenants (deals) with mankind move toward God's final deal.

> God pays everything—you pay nothing.
> You get God—and God gets you.
> Such a Deal!

God demands the only payment that will ever work to absolve the guilt in your life and plug you back in to a personal relationship with Him—death! The penalty for your sin (self-centered rebellion) is death (eternal separation from God). Either you die for eternity (which is a long time) or you allow God to make the payment through His promised Deliverer—Jesus, the Messiah.

The Bible puts it this way:

> But God demonstrates His own love toward us, in that while we were yet sinners, Christ died for us.
>
> Romans 5:8

> For there is one God, and one mediator also between God and men, the man Christ Jesus.
>
> 1 Timothy 2:5

This is why Jesus claimed, "I am the way, and the truth, and the life; no one comes to the Father, but through Me" (John 14:6). He died once for the sins of all that He might plug us back in to a relationship with God (1 Peter 3:18).

The Payoff

Most people have some idea that God has a plan for them (however elusive it may be), that mankind has sinned against God and man (no matter what you call it), and that Jesus—claiming to be the God-Man—was born on Christmas, died on Good Friday, and resurrected on Easter to take away (payment) the sins of the world. But obviously knowing these things isn't enough. You must somehow appropriate God's payment for you personally.

Let's go back to our mythical forty-foot canyon again (after recovering from our jump). Since we cannot jump it, we must find a bridge. Jesus of Nazareth, the God-Man, is the only One who can span the forty feet. He has bridged the great gap between God and man. Let's say that we just admire the bridge and discuss how truly remarkable it is—nothing happens. There is no supernatural transference from one side to the other without actually getting on the bridge.

We must cross over that bridge. Realizing that we cannot make an adequate payment for the sin that separates us from God, and that the only adequate payment is the death of Christ (the God-Man), we must receive His payment on our behalf. *That's* getting on the bridge—personally counting on and receiving God's payment for your sin. It's as if a pardon were offered to a criminal on death row. He can accept it or reject it, but it will not affect his life unless he actually receives it for himself. When we receive God's payment for sin, the payoff is made.

My favorite verses in the Bible were written by John. They explain how to receive the payment—how to plug back in to a personal relationship with God.

> For God so loved the world, that He gave His only begotten Son, that whoever believes in Him should not perish, but have eternal life.
>
> John 3:16

> But as many as received Him, to them He gave the right [authority or power] to become children of God, even to those who believe in His name.
>
> John 1:12

Receiving God's payment is the same as believing in Jesus as your Higher Power. It's trusting in Him as your personal payment for your sin against both God and man. Receiving is the simple expression of faith (getting on the bridge). It's placing all that you know you are, into all that you know He is and has done for you.

Most people receive Jesus as their Higher Power

through the process of elimination—*nothing else works!* Millions have done this by expressing their faith through a simple prayer. Prayer is talking with God. If you want the payoff of being plugged in to a personal relationship with God, say the following prayer. If you mean it, God promises to bring you in to a personal relationship with Him.

> Dear God, I confess that I have been trying to live my life unplugged from You. I realize that my self-centered rebellion (my sin—my shortcomings) must be paid for by death. I don't want to pay for it myself. I can't! So right now I want You to be my Higher Power. I want to accept Your payment of Jesus' death for me. Thank You for sending Your Deliverer for me. Amen.

Now, once you have sincerely prayed that prayer don't expect the clouds to part and a thunderous voice to break through to congratulate you or angelic wings to begin sprouting. Visible signs such as these will not be a part of your experience. But there will be many invisible changes that will have real visible impact in your life and in the lives of those around you! Most people experience a genuine inner peace, as if a load has been lifted. In many cases that load is all too real. Many experience a new love for people. Sometimes this love extends to the last person on earth they ever thought of loving!

When you pray the prayer of faith, God Himself comes to live in your life through His Spirit. All of your problems will not be solved, but you are now related to Jesus, the Problem-Solver. Your life will not always be rosy, but it'll be more meaningful and fulfilled. Jesus, as your Higher Power, is high enough to make a major difference in your life!

Part V
Straighten Up!

Step #8   *Made a list of all persons we had harmed, and became willing to make amends to them all.*

Step #9   *Made direct amends to such people wherever possible, except when to do so would injure them or others.*

9
Solicit
Forgiveness

Although this section of the book will be the shortest, it is potentially the most lethal of all! In the first four action-steps I have offered, you must face either yourself or God:

Fess Up (self)
Look Up (God)
Clean Up (self)
Give Up (God)

Now it's time to turn the corner a bit and focus your attention on others: the relationships of the past and present. First, you must make amends to those you have harmed in some way. According to Step #8 of the Twelve Steps it is time for the next action-step: Straighten Up!

> #8 *Made a list of all persons we had harmed, and became willing to make amends to them all.*

How have we harmed these people? It seems there are basically two ways in which we harm other people. The first is *commission*. Commission is that which you did or said that has harmed others, whether you meant to or not. The second is *omission*. Omission is that which you neglected to do or say that has harmed others. This one is not as easy to monitor.

Damaged relationships litter the unresolved pasts of most people I have ever met. This wreckage of relationships, whether through commission or omission, leaves millions of people injured and disfigured. We have all experienced this destruction in some way. And we have all played the part of the destroyer from time to time. The twisted and distorted lives of those who have been harmed cry out for some kind of healing and resolution.

It's time to Straighten Up, and the first step is to solicit forgiveness!

How to Solicit Forgiveness

Make Amends With Clarity

When you make amends with the people you have harmed, you must strive to do it with as much clarity as possible. First, make your list of people you know you have harmed. You can only deal with those you *know* you have harmed. It's impractical to try to imagine whom you might have harmed along the way. Start with those you know about. Others may come to mind as you work through the process.

Second, write out what you want to say to them. The wording is very significant. There are three necessary components:

1. Your *realization* that you have harmed them
2. Your *remorse* over their hurt that you caused
3. Your request for their forgiveness

It might go something like this: "I've come to realize that I have hurt you by _____. [Fill in the blank with whatever it may have been.] I feel bad about what I have done. Would you please forgive me?" Be sure to include each of the ingredients listed above.

Third, be as honest as you can. If you are not completely honest, they will be able to smell it. More than anything else your credibility hinges on this.

Fourth, be specific. You are not soliciting forgiveness in general. You can't just say, "I have come to realize that I have hurt you in some way. I feel so bad about whatever I did, so please forgive me." That doesn't get the job done. Therefore, you must be as specific and as concrete as you can be.

Fifth, keep it simple. Although it is extremely important to be as specific as you can be, don't present a seminar to the person you have harmed. Keep it as simple as possible—it's clearer.

Sixth, take personal responsibility for your actions. Don't say, "I have come to realize that I have harmed you (in the following way), but I did this harmful thing in reaction to what you had already done to me earlier." When you are soliciting forgiveness, you must focus only on the narrow one-way street of what you did to harm this person—and that's *all!*

Make Amends No Matter the Consequences

You must be willing to face any and all consequences when you decide to make amends. You may have to face ridicule, criticism, legal recourse, relational reactions, or negative financial impact!

The first time I taught through the Anyone Anonymous series, an older gentleman wrote down where he was stuck. He was a liar, a fraud. In his early twenties he was serving in the military during the Korean War. One weekend he was away from the base on a bogus pass. Several other men had done this frequently without any repercussions, but on this particular weekend his company shipped out with no prior notice! So, when he returned to the base, his bag was all that remained of his company. He panicked, and in his confusion he ran, and he kept running for over thirty years under an assumed name and new Social Security number. His running separated him from his parents and immediate family. And up until he heard this series he had not told another living soul about it—not his wife, not his kids, not anyone.

Tired of running, carrying the heavy load of guilt, and becoming physically ill from it all, he came to me looking for some relief. He had already counted the cost before we even discussed it. The military doesn't look kindly upon those who have gone AWOL—especially during time of war—but fortunately there *is* a happy ending to this story. After much frustration and many false starts in trying to take the right direction in this matter, he squarely faced the consequences. The military has treated him with great sensitivity and care. His case is soon to be resolved, and already I can see in his face the major relief of making amends.

Make Amends Completely

The most common means of soliciting forgiveness is through personal interaction, a personal telephone call, and finally a personal letter. The more personal the methods, the more effective the communication can be.

Continually I am presented with the problem of trying to solicit forgiveness from someone who is either lost (you have no address for them) or dead (even an address would not be helpful). So, what can you do? You know you have harmed this person, but there is no way to contact him. On many occasions I have suggested the following with unusual success: Write a letter! Even if the person is dead, write a letter to him soliciting forgiveness. This exercise is primarily for you anyway. You are the one who must make amends.

A short while ago a man came to me because he was troubled over the fact that he could not communicate to his dad his sorrow over how badly he had treated him through the years. His dad had died a few months prior to our meeting and this man was extremely upset because he had not taken the opportunity to make amends with him prior to his death. In our meeting I suggested that he write a letter to his dad expressing his feelings of frustration and confess the things he had done that he felt were most harmful to his dad. He was reticent at first. But after we discussed the therapeutic value in this exercise, he was, at least, willing to try it.

I didn't have to wait until our appointment the following week to find out exactly what happened. Just two days later he called to let me know. "As I began to write the letter I felt there was no way I knew what to say. I decided to just start writing and see what came out. When I was writing only the second or third line, I burst into tears—uncontrollably!" He was shocked at this emotional response. "I really didn't realize all that was in there," he said. "Before I could express my sorrow for how I had harmed my dad, a flood of angry feelings flowed through me. I now know that this anger and pride were the very things that were keeping me from asking my dad for forgiveness!"

Talk about relief! He experienced immediate relief and release in his most inner being. This is the power of making amends with those you have harmed.

Make Amends Cautiously

There is only one caution about making amends with those you have harmed: Make direct amends wherever possible, except when to do so would injure them or others. Obviously, this is a judgment call on your part. Be sensitive to what effects the sharing of your "dirty laundry" might have upon the person you have harmed or a third party!

On the other hand, don't let this be a stumbling block or an excuse that keeps you from facing the painful act of making amends with people you have harmed. It's very easy to build up faulty expectations about the effect your making amends might have on others. "If I told him that, he would kill me!" "If I open up about what I did to her, she would die of a heart attack!" "If I were to be honest about my actions, our relationship would be terminated for sure." It's been my experience that most people and relationships are not nearly as fragile as we expect them to be! In fact, being open and honest with people at the gut level of communication will most often produce a whole new level of intimacy. It's always painful, but always effective.

The Cost Factor

Many centuries ago, along a hillside, the most powerful seminar ever was delivered. The seminar was free, the speaker was a man named Jesus, and the principles were the most profound and pragmatic ever uttered. In one portion of that seminar, Jesus zeroed in on the cost factor of not seeking to solicit forgiveness.

His point was simple and specific when He said,

> If therefore you are presenting your offering at the altar, and there remember that your brother has something against you, leave your offering there before the altar, and go your way; first be reconciled to your brother, and then come and present your offering.
>
> Matthew 5:23, 24

Before you can go to God in an effective manner, you must solicit forgiveness from those you have harmed.

The cost factor? Without soliciting forgiveness you cannot work well for God!

This is the first step to Straighten Up your relationships. Now, let's move on to the vital second step.

10
You Go First

Upon further examination of that potent seminar delivered centuries ago you will discover an undergirding principle with respect to the vital act of soliciting forgiveness from those you have harmed. This underlying principle takes precedence over the first one and is absolutely necessary in order to Straighten Up your relationships! Jesus put it this way, "For if you forgive men for their transgressions, your heavenly Father will also forgive you. But if you do not forgive men, then your Father will not forgive your transgressions" (Matthew 6:14, 15).

To Straighten Up you must do two things with your relationships. First, you must solicit forgiveness from those you have harmed. Second, you must forgive those who have harmed you. If you thought the first step was the most difficult, you are in for a big surprise. This act of forgiving others who have harmed you is one of the toughest of all!

The Cost Factor

The cost factor in this principle is the most lethal. In the first step, if you don't solicit forgiveness, you can't work well for God. But in this second step, if you don't forgive, you will not be forgiven. In other words, God will not work well for you! He will not work on your behalf. The principle is simple and unequivocal—don't forgive and you don't get forgiveness.

What Is Forgiveness?

In my opinion, the most powerful and useful book on this subject of forgiveness is *Forgive and Forget* by Lewis Smedes. It has been especially helpful in clarifying my thinking on this matter. I use it continually in my counseling work and recommend it freely to everyone struggling with this need to forgive. My orientation in this area has been greatly molded by Dr. Smedes's thinking.

Let's first consider what forgiveness is *not*. Forgiveness does not mean excusing, overlooking, or tolerating another's hurtful action toward you. You may excuse, overlook, or tolerate another's hurtful behavior for a time, but there is a point at which you will have had enough. At this point you will feel the need to drag out all of the offenses you have excused, overlooked, or tolerated and use them to build an even greater case against your "enemy." When you examine it more closely, you'll come to realize that you really didn't excuse, overlook, or tolerate the actions in the first place, but merely stored them away without any resolution whatsoever. This storeroom will inevitably turn into a seething cauldron of poison that will be directed toward others or will be turned inward and be harmful to your own self! You must forgive instead of excusing, overlooking, or tolerating.

Forgiving does not mean *forgetting*. Many people seem to be stuck right here. Since they are unable to forget, they either refuse to make the effort to forgive or they become convinced that they have not really forgiven after all. Either way nullifies what forgiveness is all about. You may forgive without forgetting!

The most helpful way for me to explain forgiveness is by using the three stages Dr. Lewis Smedes suggests. The first is *hurt*. When someone harms you, it hurts. Don't try to deny it. On the contrary, when you feel that hurt, get into those feelings—moan, groan, cry from the depths of your being. Flowing with the hurt will move you along through the stages. So, feel the hurt, but don't stop here. To remain at this stage is to wallow in your hurt.

The second stage is *hate*. This, too, is most common. The anger that rises up from the hurt is only natural. Don't be afraid of it. Again, flow with it; feel the anger and express it appropriately. Experiencing the reality of your anger is also helpful in moving you through these stages. But don't stop here either. To remain at this stage is to fester your hate.

The third stage is *healing!* This stage requires a decision on your part to bear the pain yourself. Making it through to this stage frees the perpetrator of the pain from your vengeance and frees you, the victim, from the certain damage and destruction that will come from wallowing in your hurt and letting your hate fester.

The results you experience from your act of forgiving those who have harmed you may not be all you expected them to be. Naturally you hope for some kind of relational resolve with the one who has harmed you, a reconciliation of some kind. But although you may work toward and hope for this positive result, it just may not be what actually happens. And you must be prepared for that. The person may not acknowledge your efforts at all. You may find yourself completely rejected or even ridiculed for taking this vulnerable and noble action of forgiving. Their positive response is not necessary for your forgiveness to be effective. Remember, you are not doing this as a performance to be graded by another person; you are doing this primarily for yourself. No one else can do it for you. No one can Straighten Up your relationships by the use of the forgiveness dynamic but you!

How to Forgive

1. Remind Yourself They're Only Humans

Those who have harmed you are only human. We tend to treat people like the fallible humans they are, until one of them hurts us. Then, we are shocked and horrified over their actions! You must see them again as part of the human race with all of its shortcomings—especially when they have harmed you.

2. Relinquish Your Right to Get Even

It's so natural to attempt to even the score in some way. When you are hurt, you want to get back at someone. A few weeks ago a friend of mine expressed this when he said, "I don't get mad. I get even!"

I realized quite a while ago that it's impossible to get even. There is no way you can exactly duplicate for someone else the pain you feel. Either you will not give them enough pain to equal yours or you will overdo the pain, giving them much more than you experienced and thus producing the classic feud where the fighting is endless and most destructive. You can't really get even, so don't even try!

3. Be Ready to Hurt in Order to Heal

To me, this is the heart and soul of forgiveness: You must be willing to take the pain and bear it alone. This is the most God-like quality you'll ever be challenged to perform. To forgive, you must be willing to bear the pain alone without any strings of revenge attached.

4. Really Wish Them Well

Genuine forgiveness requires this. Without it, your forgiveness is phony! How can you say, "I forgive them," and secretly or publicly enjoy their demise or defeat at the same time? You don't have to join their personal promotion department. You don't even have to associate with them as friends or business acquaintances. Nor am I saying that you must agree with their intentions or motivations, their goals or their methods. But you must wish them well.

This may mean you wish for them to find some help with their lives. Maybe a better way to say "wish them well" is to say "pray for them." By this, I don't mean to suggest that you have pity on them, but that you channel your anger into a genuine compassion for their well-being. This may possibly be the most freeing experience of all in forgiving those who have harmed you.

5. Repeat the Process

Forgiveness is a process. You can count on the fact that once you have forgiven someone, you may be faced with feeling the hurt and hate all over again through the various circumstances of life. Therefore, forgiveness is necessary all over again.

Jesus gave an interesting guideline as to how many times you must be willing to forgive the same person. He suggested that you should be ready to forgive as many as 490 times! Forgiveness is a process that must be repeated.

Why Forgiveness Is So Important

There are, at least, four good reasons why forgiveness is so important. The first is that you can't receive forgiveness without forgiving. Remember the principle—if you don't forgive, you will not be forgiven.

The second is that you will be under bondage to the person who hurt you in the first place. You will not have personal freedom individually or within that particular relationship. Not many years ago, I counseled a woman whose husband had left her for another woman. Obviously, she was hurt very deeply, but she was never able to move through the stages of forgiveness. Instead, she remained in the hurt and hate stages for the next six years. Whether at work or play she could not think or talk about anything else but this jerk who left her high and dry! Just last year she entered the hospital for a cancer operation. Not only has she had no life of her own since the divorce, but she has now been stricken down with the deadly disease of cancer. Talk about bondage!

The third reason forgiveness is important is that you will not experience healing without it. As you can see in the previous illustration, your own health is at great risk because of your own stubbornness to forgive. A friend of mine had a major falling-out with both his parents and then refused to ever forgive them. I watched this refusal gradually destroy him. Today, he is in and out of the hospital with a rare nervous disorder. He can hardly function with any kind of normality. If only he could have forgiven them in the past or even forgive them today as they lie in their graves. But he never would and will not now heed any prodding toward expressing forgiveness. What a sick man! What a tragic and unnecessary predicament to live in the rest of your life.

The fourth reason why it is so important to forgive is that you will not progress in your growth if you don't. Your personal growth will inevitably be stifled or stunted, at best.

This, then, is why it is so important to forgive: When you make amends, you don't do it for others. You do it for yourself!

If you don't solicit forgiveness, you can't work well for God!

If you don't forgive others, God can't work well for you!

Part VI
Keep It Up!

STEP #10   *Continued to take personal inventory and when we were wrong promptly admitted it.*

STEP #11   *Sought through prayer and meditation to improve our conscious contact with God* as we understood Him, *praying only for knowledge of His will and the power to carry that out.*

STEP #12   *Having had a spiritual awakening as the result of these steps, we tried to carry this message to others with problems, and to practice these principles in all our affairs.*

11
Relapse—Your Greatest Enemy

Years ago, I heard a story about a famous pirate. As you might expect he had several battle scars. He had a peg leg, a hook for an arm, and a patch over one eye. Toward the end of the piracy era a young reporter asked him for an interview. Reluctantly, he agreed to a meeting on his boat. When the reporter arrived, he saw a great picture. The famous pirate was sitting on the bow of his battle-torn ship with a sword drawn as if in a battle.

After the reporter had captured several shots of this scene, the interview began. "Let's start by your telling me the story behind each of your battle scars. How did you lose your leg?" The pirate moved into a hairy war story about the time he took a hit from a cannonball across the bow from an enemy ship.

"What about the arm? How did you lose it?"

"Well, in one of the toughest fights I was ever in against a rival pirate, he temporarily knocked me out. And while I was down, he took his huge sword and with one swipe severed my right arm at the elbow!"

The reporter realized he was getting good stuff, so he eagerly continued. "Tell me about the battle in which you lost your eye?"

"Oh, that wasn't a battle. That was a sea gull!"

The reporter was amazed and in shock yelled out, "A sea gull! What did he do, attack you?"

"No, one evening while I was admiring the stars in the sky, a flock of sea gulls flew over and one of them pooped a direct hit in my right eye."

"But there is no way that would put an eye out!"

The pirate quickly answered, "Well, there is when it's the first day after you get your hook!"

One of the most fascinating observations I have made as I have counseled thousands of people with thousands of problems is that most of the problems have either been caused by or made worse by the people themselves—by the use of their own hooks! It seems to be a part of the human condition. We often take the problems we have and hurt ourselves with them rather than entering into the process of genuine healing.

In the first nine of the Twelve Steps, I have offered five action-steps for your practical application of the Twelve Steps:

Twelve Steps	Action-Steps
Steps 1–2	Fess Up!
Step 3	Look Up!
Steps 4–5	Clean Up!
Steps 6–7	Give Up!
Steps 8–9	Straighten Up!

The last three of the Twelve Steps—Steps 10, 11, and 12—bring us to the last action-step—Keep It Up! Most of us are better in a crisis situation than we are in the continual follow-through of life. It also may be true that it is easier to make a commitment to die for something than it is to live for something. When it comes to processing your problem, it's one thing to correct it for the moment, but quite another to keep up the process of consistent growth and healing. In other words, once you have walked through the steps of dealing with your problem, you must learn to Keep It Up. Keeping up a life-style of growth and healing involves entering the process of total recovery, facing the problem of relapse, and becoming proactive through repossessing your life.

The Process of Total Recovery

The term *recovery* is used in a very partial manner much of the time. Unfortunately, recovery is equated to abstinence, but abstinence is not recovery. It denotes only the correction of a person's problem without the positive move toward new, healthy attitudes and actions. Abstinence by itself neglects the full understanding of the context necessary for total recovery.

The context of total recovery is the same for anyone with any kind of problem. There are five dimensions to it: physical, mental, emotional, social, and spiritual. Partial recovery is the attempt to solve your problem by the use of only a few, but not all, of these. It would be like solving an alcohol or drug problem by only physical means, solving obsessive, sick thinking by mental means alone, solving intense guilt and depression by only the emotional, solving marriage problems with social and relational principles alone, solving an eating disorder by only spiritual means.

Each of these dimensions of recovery has great truths with powerful effects. But each one contains only a part of the truth! The physical proponents believe that you must eat and exercise properly in order to live your life to the fullest, and that the physical dimension can be the key to heal you completely. The mental proponents believe that what you need is to have a clearer perspective and more educated thinking with respect to your problem—then you will enjoy a full and meaningful life. The emotional proponents believe that you must get in tune with your gut-level feelings and learn to express them appropriately. They feel this is the path to living your life with unusual satisfaction and fulfillment. The social proponents believe that the key to life is handling your relationships more effectively—past, present, and future—and that through this dimension you will be boosted into the fullness of life. The spiritual proponents believe that the spiritual dimension is the primary key to life. If you are centered into your spiritual being, you can overcome and work through anything.

Each one of these dimensions contains truth, but it is only partial truth. You must have all five working together in a "full court press" against the problem in order to move into total recovery.

It's like five blind men trying to describe an elephant. One has the elephant's tail, the second an ear, another a foot, another the trunk, and the fifth is holding on to a tusk. As each one records his experience, he is telling the truth, but it is only partial truth. The tail, ear, foot, trunk, or the tusk is not the whole elephant. What is needed is for all the partial truths to be integrated into a whole for us to begin to get the picture of what an elephant looks like. This is what is needed in the world of recovery. We need a description of the whole elephant! This is what I mean by total recovery.

The Problem of Relapse

Now that you have walked your problem through the first nine steps of the Twelve Steps, the worst possible thing that could happen would be for you to fall into the same old routine again. This horrible return into the same old problem-driven life-style is known as *relapse*.

If you haven't already begun to relapse, you will. It's like taking one step forward and two steps back. It's very likely that most people who are reading this book are already on the skids to relapse right now. And if you are, you know it deep down inside.

Many times this plunge into relapse is an indicator that you are in need of something else in your attempt at total recovery. But relapse is always a threat to you and could easily happen. You must be ready for it, so that you are not taken by surprise.

The Setup

Relapse always begins long before the crisis. The setup for relapse is subtle, yet lethal, because it will surely take you for a wild ride back into big trouble. Too often this trouble is much bigger than that which you experienced originally!

There are, at least, four common setups for relapse. The first is that expectations often exceed reality. When your expectations are too high, you are in for a major jolt of raw and shocking reality that will create painful disappointment within. Expectations are normally impossible to accurately experience anyway. Expectations of being happier than you've ever been before or feeling good about yourself or finally experiencing success do not have enough tangibility to them to be measured. They are simply too subjective! Subjective expectations are easily destroyed: Happiness can be destroyed by some sad news; feeling good about yourself can be destroyed by a three-pound weight gain; and the experience of success can be destroyed by a failure or two. The key to nullifying this setup is to close the gap between your expectations and reality. Lower your expectations and increase your perspective on reality.

The second setup is the thought that willpower alone will get you through. This bit of false thinking will set you up royally to slide right into a relapse experience. I have noticed that dieters have the strongest willpower of all. But when they finally give in to the temptation to go for the chocolate brownie or the bag of candy, the dam seems to break! Up until the dam breaks there are few people on the face of the earth who exhibit more willpower than the professional dieter. The point must be driven home strongly that willpower alone will not get you through the battle with your problem—it's a trick, a setup!

The third setup for relapse is to think that recovery is not that tough. Most of us look at life this way. We see what we have been running from and what we are running to, but miss out on the process. Perception of what it takes to turn away from an old habit pattern and translate that into something healthy and profitable is blurry and limited at best. Now that I've been into the recovery world for several years personally and professionally, I'm convinced that recovery is the most difficult life-process you could ever enter into. Recovery may just be the toughest move of your life!

The fourth setup is the belief that short-term results equal successful recovery. It's so easy to be fooled by the good feelings you experience from the little positive results along the road to recovery. A month without a drink! Two weeks without sugar! Blood pressure down to a healthy level for the first time in ten years! Your marriage going so well you're afraid to wake up! These and many more positive, short-term results can be the foolers that falsely communicate to you that you are doing too well to ever go back to that old destructive life-style! But as the famous proverb says, "Pride comes before a fall. . . ." With this attitude the fall of relapse becomes inevitable. Enjoy the short-term results, but go for the long-term, quality stuff!

The Stages of Relapse

Stage #1—Complacency   The first stage, complacency, occurs when humility is replaced by self-reliance. The cover-up and dishonesty that characterized your life earlier return for a reunion of sorts. At this stage you'll find yourself saying things like, "I don't need to go to meetings anymore," or, "I don't need to keep working through the steps anymore," or, "I just don't need to press as intensely as I had to before." Essentially, when you find yourself slipping back into any form of denial—even the slightest bit— you are into the first stage of relapse!

Stage #2—Confusion   In the second stage, confusion, confidence is replaced by doubt. You progressively doubt the need for any sort of help. There is also a serious doubt about the severity of your problem in the first place. At this stage you'll be saying, "My problem really wasn't that bad after all." Comparison becomes the constant theme to the point of justifying yourself—"In comparison to him, I'm not as bad as I thought." This is the point where the alcoholic says to himself, *A little wine wouldn't hurt.* The overeater's self-talk is, *One candy bar wouldn't hurt.* And the gambler is thinking, *Just a look at the racing form wouldn't hurt.* The confusion is caused by a series of contradictions that are bouncing around in your head about your condition.

Stage #3—Compromise   In the third stage, compromise, vulnerability is replaced by the illusion of control. You'll find yourself stuck trying to prove all is under control. Therefore, you'll put yourself in risky situations to meet the test. You'll say things like, "I'm just going to the tavern for a Coke." When you begin to take these risks to test how strong you are, you are well on your way down the road to relapse.

Stage #4—Calamity   In the fourth and last stage of relapse, calm and confidence are replaced by chaos and catastrophe. Though this final stage seems to happen all of a sudden, it really doesn't. It's the result of a predictable progression of choices, each of which is usually precipitated by the temptation for momentary gratification. But to choose this temporary route to satisfaction produces everything except what you intended. Unfortunately, the product created is an intense, long-term guilt and shame. "Here I am again, back where I used to be!" To fall down while you are progressing on the road to wholeness can send you into discouragement real fast! That's the calamity of it all. Let's quickly move on to some preventive measures before discouragement settles into depression.

The Prevention of Relapse

What is really necessary here is to get into the driver's seat of your life so that you are becoming proactive rather than reactive. What you need is a daily game plan for living your life. Each of the last three steps (#10 to #12) offers a helpful guideline for such a plan. I refer to this proactive plan as repossessing your life! Let's consider each one carefully.

Step #10 *We continued to take personal inventory and when we were wrong promptly admitted it.*

The daily guideline in this step is to recognize your problem areas—every day. In a very real sense, the regular recognition of your problem areas is a continual process of working through the principles of the first nine of the Twelve Steps. It's a continual recognition that you have a problem, you're powerless over it, and your life has become unmanageable because of it. It's a continual recognition of a Power greater than yourself to whom you must turn over your will and your life for His care and direction. It's continually going in for major moral surgery and asking God to remove all of your shortcomings. It's continually looking to make amends to those you have harmed by soliciting forgiveness and forgiving those who have harmed you.

This is the review step of problem orientation! To Keep It Up you must keep your problem in perspective—each and every day! You soon realize that you can't turn your back on what has brought you this far. Keeping your problem areas ever before you, helps you to handle your life with greater balance and perspective. Your progress in life is dependent upon living your life in process.

Step #11 *We sought through prayer and meditation to improve our conscious contact with God as we understood Him,* *praying only for knowledge of His will for us and the power to carry that out.*

The daily guideline in this step is to renew your relationship with God—every day. Without this regular reminder that God wants to be intimately involved in a personal relationship with you, it's too easy to shift into "playing God" on your own. It's a natural tendency to-ward leaving God out of things.

In the American society we do this all the time. Take Santa Claus, for instance. Little boys grow up believing in Santa. As they grow older they don't believe in him any-more. Then, when these little boys grow up to be big boys (fathers), they begin to believe that they *are* Santa Claus! We do that with God as well. As youngsters we believe in God. As we grow older, we tend to not believe in God. And then later on, as we enter adulthood, we believe we are God!

You must Keep It Up by renewing your relationship with God each and every day. This is the review step of power for personal renewal. You can plug yourself in to the power you need for personal renewal. By this I cer-tainly don't mean that you must turn into some kind of religious fanatic! It's just a simple maintenance of this new-found relationship you have with God so that you are always aware of your need to be plugged in to His care and power. Read selected passages out of the Bible—Psalms, Proverbs, stories of how God worked in the lives of others in the past, and so on. Pray to Him concerning your life, your loved ones, and your livelihood. Listen to Him by taking the time to meditate alone—just to be quiet and listen. All of this will keep you from making only emergency calls to God. Instead, you'll be relating with Him every day. Then, when the next emergency arises, you won't have to go off looking for Him, He'll already be there!

Step #12   *Having had a spiritual awakening as the result of these steps, we tried to carry this message to other people with problems, and to practice these principles in all our affairs.*

The daily guideline in this step is to reach out to someone in need—every day. There is nothing—no therapy, no seminar, no book, no formula—that is more helpful to your own growth and recovery than to become meaningfully involved in helping someone else! This step completes the cycle of recovery.

We are such needy people, that we grab for everything we can get for ourselves rather than to give ourselves away toward meeting another's need. All day long, each and every day, there are people around you who are in need. If you don't make a move to help them, who will? Turn your head and your heart toward reaching out to someone in need. This is the review step of people restoration. You can make a significant difference in your world by helping to restore people to a healthy life-style. In the next chapter we'll pursue this vital dynamic more extensively.

Steps 10, 11, and 12 are the necessary ingredients to Keep It Up. By applying Step 10 to you personally, Step 11 to your relationship with God, and Step 12 to your efforts to help the "others" in your life, you are doing the things that are absolutely required to repossess your life.

One Day at a Time

There is one more critical thought that will change your life forever when understood and applied. Notice that you are to recognize your problem areas—*every day;* renew your relationship with God—*every day;* and reach out to someone in need—*every day.* In other words, you must learn to live your life *one day at a time!*

One day at a time is the most important principle I know for living life to the fullest and with the wisest perspective. You were never intended to live your life any other way. Anyone can make it through just one day at a time.

Jesus taught this principle long before the Twelve Steps were written. He said, "Therefore, do not be anxious for tomorrow; for tomorrow will care for itself. Each day has enough trouble of its own" (Matthew 6:34). In fact, this principle was taught to the Jewish people as they were wandering in the wilderness. God fed the people of Israel a food called manna which was to be gathered on a daily basis—no more and no less. He fed them every day—one day at a time! Jesus' words are most interesting. "Do not be anxious for tomorrow. . . ." There is no wiser statement. I know that when I think about tomorrow, I immediately become anxious. When I think about what I must face this coming week, my cholesterol level must jump fifty points. The people I am scheduled to see. The deadlines I face. The eight times I must lecture this week on five different topics in four different cities. The bills that are due. How can you *not* be anxious when you think of tomorrow? His point in saying this is not to get you to avoid any thoughts or plans for your tomorrows, but to get you through this one day, today—*one day at a time.*

How many times have you said to yourself, *I don't believe I'll ever get through this week!* But you did! Oh, I know, you may have felt a little damaged by it, but you did make it through. Anyone can make it through until midnight. You can beat any problem, if you only have to hang in there until midnight. Then, when you awaken in the morning you discover that you made it through another day. And today, all you have to do is hang in there until midnight again. Try it. Live your life one day at a time.

12
From Recovery
to Discovery

Over the years I have been especially concerned about what I have seen as a trap within recovery. Now, I realize that I have spent the entire book trying to move you into recovery, but within even the best recovery there is a desperate problem that more and more people are experiencing. What I am describing is a form of being stuck, but this time it's being stuck in the state of recovery itself. That's right, you can even be stuck in your own recovery!

You are stuck in recovery when your whole identity is wrapped up in being a "recovered whatever." Now, there is nothing wrong with being a "recovered whatever," but there must be more to life than this—more progress—more growth—more life!

Reactive Maintenance

Once you are on the road to recovery, there are two approaches to living your life. The first is *reactive mainte-*

nance. With this approach your primary goal is to stay "clean and sober" with respect to your problem—to survive. Growth becomes just holding on to life itself. Naturally, this feels so much better than being stuck in a destructive cycle. It's certainly better than slipping and sliding on the downward spiral you were on. But when your primary focus and energy are channeled only toward maintaining a clean and sober state, there are a couple of common problems that threaten your continued growth and happiness.

One very common trap is to wallow in your problem. If your constant focus and energy are on your problem, you will easily slip into being problem-oriented and *that* becomes your problem! This wallowing around produces a stagnation and frequently triggers a low-grade depression about your life. And when you are not excited about your life, you are highly vulnerable to return to the clutches of your old problem or other related problems. Obviously, this can become a sure setup for falling back to square one or lower!

Another very common problem in the maintenance approach is to contemplate your own navel! To wallow was to be problem-oriented; to contemplate your own navel is to be *me*-oriented. This one is the natural result of the other. You start with "look how bad I have it with my problem" and end with "poor me." When you are into a "poor me" syndrome, you place yourself in a victim role which, in turn, makes you most vulnerable to personal destruction.

Both of these common problems are extremely selfish in their inner-directedness. Given this self-centered, survival approach, your downfall is inevitable! People are created to be both inner- and outer-directed for their own well-being. For best results you must learn to live inside out!

It's this balance between the personal and the interpersonal that makes for the highest quality growth!

Proactive Movement

The reactive maintenance approach doesn't work. The second approach is *proactive movement*. The primary goal of this approach is to move your life toward personal growth and development—to stretch yourself. There is little wallowing, only a willingness to learn and change. There is little contemplation of your navel, only significant contributions to the world around you.

This is what I call going from recovery to discovery! Recovery was never intended to be an arrival point in your life, but a continual process of discovery. Several years ago I was hit with a very practical insight on how to ensure the possibility of living life to the fullest. Not only has this been unusually helpful in the counseling room, but it has also proved to be most vital in my own life. In order to stretch yourself into this life-discovery mode you must insist upon three vital proactive relationships. I use the word *insist* because these relationships are so crucial to your growth and happiness. The three relationships to which I'm referring are three types of action relationships—takers, giver/takers, and givers.

The Taker Relationship

The first of these vital, proactive relationships is the taker relationship. Now this may sound a little selfish, a little greedy, or even non-Christian. And by itself, the taker relationship *is* all of the above—selfish, greedy, and non-Christian. But, functioning as one of the three types of action relationships it becomes a necessary ingredient to stretch you into healthy discovery.

You must insist upon retaining a taker relationship through which you take in life-sustaining information and energy. This may be accomplished through reading good literature, listening to audio tapes, viewing video tapes, attending seminars and workshops, sitting at the feet of a mentor/teacher, participating in a small support group, and so on. You must be in a relationship in which you are able to build up your storehouse of emotional and mental reserves.

It's a relationship through which you are *being ministered to* personally. You see, there is a basic fact of life that says you cannot give anything away unless you possess it yourself. But if you avoid this relationship, you will be running on empty most of your life. Unfortunately, this is where the majority of people live their lives most often—on empty!

The Giver/Taker Relationship

The second of these vital, proactive relationships is the giver/taker relationship. This is just as vital and, in many respects, just as rare as the first. This relationship is a two-way street on which you are *ministering alongside* another person. There must be giving and taking between (at least) two people.

This kind of relationship is rare today—especially among men. The giver/taker relationship requires a mutual risk. It's like placing your head on the chopping block, handing the ax to your friend, and letting him do as he wills with it. There is also a mutual sharing. One of the great values of being in a relationship with another person is that you not only share your own life experiences, feelings, and thoughts, but you also learn to share someone else's burdens. In this way mutual sharing becomes a mutual support. Nothing is more potent than this kind of mutuality. It's a wonderful feeling to know that someone is out there who gives a rap whether you live or die.

Years ago, thinking that one of our partners needed some counseling, we hired two psychiatrists to examine each of us with extensive testing. When it was my turn to be reviewed by the doctors, I was shocked and a bit overwhelmed by what they told me: They strongly suggested that I begin to establish some peer relationships with other men in order to be able to process my own inner feelings. They scared me to death! That very week, over sixteen years ago, I began the practice of establishing for myself several giver/taker relationships. It's a good feeling to have the support of a few others who not only give a rap whether you live or die, but are also willing to tell you when you're full of it! You'll come to the point where you won't be able to live without this kind of relationship.

The Giver Relationship

This relationship completes the cycle of the discovery mode. You must have a taker relationship, a giver/taker relationship, and a giver relationship. This relationship brings a wholesomeness and balance to your life—an unusually healthy perspective. In the taker relationship you need to be ministered to, in the giver/taker relationship you need to be ministering alongside of, and in the giver relationship you *minister to others.*

When I'm able to get a person into the giver relationship, it is a powerfully effective therapy and there is no substitute for it. There is nothing more effective for an alcoholic than to help another person whip alcohol . . . for parents who have lost their children to death to stand with other parents in the same situation . . . for the woman who was molested in her childhood to empathize with a recent victim of molestation . . . for the person motivated by love to intervene into a friend's problem. Not only is this the most credible help the hurting person can receive, but it is the most healing activity the giver can experience.

People helping other people (friends, acquaintances, and family) in their unique area of hurt (people suffering similar pains) is the most natural matchup possible. The amazing thing about this kind of matchup is that it doesn't have to be artificially or professionally set up. Most of these matchups are already set up through the normal relationships you possess and the networking possibilities that result from these same relationships. It's like they're miraculously set up!

Divine Appointments

Over the years I've come to identify these seemingly miraculous matchups as divine appointments. Divine appointments are set up for us every day of our lives. All we have to do is show up. There are three kinds of appointments. The first are the *scheduled appointments*. These are the appointments that are on your calendar. To some degree, you know them and either set them up yourself or accepted their initiation by someone else. Although there may be a stated reason for the scheduled appointment, you end up giving yourself instead to meet a real need in that person's life.

The second kind of divine appointment is the *spontaneous appointment*. This happens when you run into a person you know and that person has a problem and all of a sudden, you're there to meet it.

The third kind are the *surprise appointments*. Surprise appointments are those people you bump into during your day whom you did not previously know. This might be on the plane, in the restaurant, or any kind of situation where you could meet people. The overall goal of the giver relationship is to make a difference in people's lives which, in turn, makes a major difference in you.

There isn't any greater therapy. It helps you to remove the unhealthy focus on yourself and your problem. It demonstrates that you are not the only one with a problem— and, in most cases, your problem isn't nearly as bad when you are giving yourself away. It gives you a sense of doing something worthwhile. *It's life-changing for you.*

There isn't any greater healing. People all around you are dying in a pile. Many you know. Many more you haven't a clue about. But if you listen carefully, you can become more aware of the problems of those around you and of the role you can play in their potential healing. *It's life-changing for others.*

Divine Appointments Begin in the Morning

The way you start your day will determine how well you operate in the giver relationship with the divine appointments. You basically have two options: First, you can wake up saying, "Good morning, God. What do You have for me to do today?" This attitude alone will produce positive results for your day. When you start your day in this manner, you are already more aware of looking for the people in need (the divine appointments) in your world and you'll enjoy your day immensely!

The second way you can start your day is to wake up saying, "Good God! It's morning!" Start your day like this and you are in for a miserable day! Everything seems like an interruption—every call, every appointment, every meeting. You spend your day running from the opportunities to give yourself to others in need and hating every minute of it.

When I wake up with "Good morning, God. What do You have for me to do today?" I seem to be filled with divine appointments all day long! Just last week I had one of those surprise divine appointments. I had just left a basketball meeting at the local Boys Club and was on my way to speak to a small group of musicians. Since my next meeting was only a few miles away and I had a little extra time, I decided to make a quick stop at a local department store to look for a shirt. While looking for a parking space, I noticed a man being very abusive to a lady who was walking with him. First he was yelling at her, then he hit her and shoved her into the wall of the department store. I put my window down and yelled, "What's the problem?" Needless to say, the man was not thrilled with my interruption. With a few choice words, he started toward my car. Then I yelled out to the woman, "You don't have to take that, you know." When I said this, the woman quickly moved toward me and exclaimed, "You're my pastor!" With this, the man seemed to be taken aback and darted off through the parking lot. I was able to help her get to her car, and then I offered her some advice on what to do with her "hot date." Now, that was a divine appointment!

While doing some writing in a local restaurant one afternoon, I noticed a man, woman, and young girl seated at the table next to me. The little girl was fidgeting around and knocked her drink over, splashing my table pretty thoroughly. The woman immediately grabbed the girl and began to whale on her. The man snapped, "Are you going to beat her like you do at home?" That seemed a pretty strange thing to say. And the woman was visibly shaken by his comments!

I had the waitress get the girl another drink and set her up at my table, and I moved over to their table. "It sounds like there are some problems here," I said. And the man answered, "Yeah, and she's got 'em!" It turned out that the man was her brother and the mother of the girl was engaging in some uncontrollable beatings of her daughter. Within forty-eight hours I was able to get her some much-needed help for her problem. Wouldn't you call that a divine appointment?

A few days ago I had an appointment with an executive who lives in our area. We were to discuss a community issue that had become quite controversial and divisive. We spent most of our luncheon time on that particular issue, but I sensed an uneasiness about this man. So, after we had nearly exhausted our discussion of the issue at hand, I turned to him and asked, "How are you doing personally?"

I couldn't believe the floodgate that opened up! He unloaded on me his great concerns for his marriage and one of his teenagers. The emotional tension in this man was hard to believe. He had always presented himself as "having it all together," but this time he was most vulnerable and in need of someone to lean on. Every appointment—even the most normal ones—can turn into a divine appointment.

During the week of October 15, 1989, my wife, Carol, and I flew to San Francisco and checked into the Westin St. Francis Hotel in the downtown area near Union Square. I was scheduled to speak on Tuesday afternoon, October 16, at 3:15 P.M., and also at a Wednesday morning prayer breakfast and at two more sessions over the next two days. I felt unusually troubled as to why I was at this conference. I was especially concerned about speaking at the afternoon slot, because I couldn't imagine how anyone would attend a meeting at that time of day. Before I left for the afternoon session, I told Carol that I felt ambivalent about the entire conference and yet I knew God must have some good reason for my speaking there—even at three-fifteen in the afternoon!

I was surprised at the turnout for the dreaded afternoon session. It really went quite well, after all. I finished about four-thirty, made a few calls from the lobby, and took the elevator up to the eighteenth floor. As soon as I stepped off the elevator, a 7.1 earthquake hit! The hotel tower shook and swayed back and forth! As I made my way down the hall to our room I heard a lady crying and screaming, "We're going to die! We're all going to die!"

Living in California, I have experienced several earthquakes, but this one was more powerful and much longer than anything I had ever experienced before. With the incredible movement of the building and the woman's predictions in the background, I began to think, *She's right!* I was sure that this quake was going to topple the building and we could possibly die in this one!

I finally made it to our room, where I found Carol and we waited out the last few seconds of the quake. As soon as it was over, we both knew why we were at that conference! We quickly went back down the hall to assist the terrified woman I'd heard. Comforting her was the first in a whole list of divine appointments waiting for us to show up! Needless to say, attendance at the following morning's prayer breakfast nearly doubled—even without electricity and water. It was appointment after appointment for the next twenty-four hours. What a trip!

The interesting thing about divine appointments is that you don't have to know a whole lot to show up at them.

The main thing is to make sure you are there. I heard a terrific principle a few years ago—Wherever you are, be *all* there! This is all that's necessary for these vital, divine appointments.

In going from recovery to discovery you must insist upon three relationships for your life—the taker, the giver/taker, and the giver.

Part VII
Now What?

13
Your Self-Esteem Is All You've Got!

There is an old Scottish prayer that says, "Lord, grant that we may always be right. For Thou knowest we will never change our minds." The stubbornness within human beings is amazing. Even when the results aren't very satisfying, you can count on people to stubbornly make the same destructive decision over and over again!

A man read in the paper about a cruise for only $100, so he quickly went to the travel agency and signed up. As soon as he signed the contract and paid his $100, a trapdoor opened up sending him down a long shoot! When he awakened from the fall, he found himself in a blue rowboat in the middle of the Pacific—on his $100 cruise! He cruised all day long and into the night. The next morning he was thrilled to see another blue rowboat cruising toward him. As they approached each other, he yelled out, "Hey, do they serve breakfast on this cruise?" The other man shrugged his shoulders and said, "I don't know. They didn't last year."

In some ways, it's laughable to see how we continually fall into making bad choices. But it's not laughable when you think of what is at stake. Undergirding every problem that we struggle with is the most serious problem of all—perceiving and preserving your self-esteem. Your self-esteem is all you've got. That's you!

In fact, the more I counsel and help people struggle through their problems, the more I'm convinced that lack of self-esteem is at the core of all our problems! We have more information available to us today on how to solve our problems than ever before, yet it seems that all of these problems are becoming increasingly worse—not better! Why are all of our cures, treatments, programs, workshops, books, tapes, and the like not working enough to make a significant difference? In my opinion, the answer to that question is that our thinking with respect to self-esteem has become blurry.

Perspective: M.O. of Man

How do you obtain value? How can you appreciate in value? The answers to these questions vary according to how the needs of man are listed. Some list three. Others say there are basically five needs. Still others would offer an even larger listing. But the *basic* needs of the human being are pretty commonly accepted.

I see three kinds of basic needs: the security needs, the social needs, and the significance needs.

The Security Needs

Man has a great need to be accepted for who he is. But we have turned this all upside down. Acceptance is readily available for your performance and accomplishments, your intelligence and appearance, and your power and position. But acceptance for who you are? That's rare!

So, to meet his security needs, man naturally goes after the things in life that are valued by society. Man tries to find happiness and security in all the wrong places.

Although *money* is presumed by many to be the most certain source of security, there are three other sources that promise happiness and security—*people, places,* and *things.* Each one of these makes promises it cannot deliver.

Many believe people can make them happy. People can contribute to another's happiness and security, but people cannot make you happy. If you give people the responsibility to make you happy and secure, then you are also giving them the right and power to cause you great unhappiness and insecurity.

Others believe places can make them happy and secure. Well, it doesn't take many counseling sessions to realize that this isn't so. I counsel people who live in mansions with an ocean view as well as those who live without a mansion or a view. Neither are happy and secure! Believe me, places do not make people happy.

Still others hold the belief that things can make you happy. The popular bumper sticker "The one who dies with the most toys wins!" expresses this approach to happiness and security. The things that make you happy and secure can also make you very miserable and insecure. In each of these—people, places, and things—a temporary happiness and sense of security is part of the package, but over the long haul, none of these can pass the test.

There is an ache within everyone which needs to be satisfied. Where will your security needs find this satisfaction?

The Social Needs

The social needs of people—the need for relationships—are even more evident than the security needs. Relational problems are more and more prevalent within marriages, families, neighborhoods, and on the job. The wreckage of relationships has virtually trashed our entire society. Approximately only one out of every nine families is a traditional family—husband and wife in their first marriage with their own children. The major portion of the nontraditional world has been created by the wreckage within our shaky relationships.

The most common way to attempt to fill this need is through some sort of sexual expression. Not only is this one of the most saturated themes in our society, it appears to be the quickest and most enjoyable way to move into some kind of intimate relationship. But, in reality, sex can easily become the quickest way to nowhere—temporarily enjoyable, but potentially lethal. Sex, more often than not, becomes the monster that cheats you out of genuine intimacy.

Intimacy is the goal of the social needs. Though intimacy is mentioned frequently in conversation, not many actually experience this illusive dynamic. Not only is the experience rare, but so is the person who knows how to be sensitive in relationships. Therefore, the divorcing, the distancing, and the damaging of relationships continues at an epidemic rate. So, where will your social needs find this sensitivity to relationships?

The Significance Needs

Why am I here? What difference do I make to this world or to anyone? Am I worthwhile? These are the questions that seem to flow out of the significance needs.

The haunting and underlying sense of destiny, a sense of purpose in life is what is lacking here. There is a longing within each one of us for a special reason for our existence. It's precisely because of this longing that people spend endless hours in search of their roots. It's why adopted children set out to find their natural parents, why every kid—young or old—loves to hear one more time the circumstances of his birth and childhood. There is something about how we are launched into this world that provides some answers about our significance.

Your significance is uniquely *you*. The unique space you fill in this world. The unique combination of strengths and weaknesses you bring to every situation. The unique role you are to play in the world around you. The unique sense of destiny—direction, purpose, and hope—that only *you* hold in your heart of hearts. But where will your significance needs find this sense of destiny?

Your security, social, and significance needs are very real and must be fulfilled somehow. Unfortunately, in most cases, these are filled up with counterfeit answers and promote a facade or mask in place of genuine self-esteem.

Problem: Model of Man

Another problem most critical to self-esteem is the nature of man. With a clear perspective of your nature in focus, a healthy picture of your self shines through. Then, and only then, can you esteem your self. Then, and only then, can you value your self—your personness. But if your self—your personness—is devalued, you lose everything, including your self!

It's not enough that your self-esteem is being attacked

by all sorts of problems—failures, victimizations, dysfunctional families, habits, and addictions, but there is another
attack upon your self-esteem that may be even more devastating. There is the attack from within the society of man
itself! There's another holocaust looming over our heads,
only this time it isn't targeted for a specific race of people,
but for the human race. Man's inhumanity to man has
been evident throughout the world as man continues to
wage war after war to exert his position and power. But
this is more insidious, more lethal to the human race. The
"man's inhumanity to man" to which I am referring is
man's dehumanizing man himself.

The Rape of Humanity

There is a crime being committed against the human
race, and there is no better description of the crime than
rape. Rape is "the act of seizing and carrying off by force"
and that is exactly what is occurring. Mankind is being
raped of its personness, and as a result, man is becoming
less than man—man is quickly becoming non-man! It's no
wonder people turn to chemicals and choose destructive
paths for their life's direction; nothing else is worth living
for—including themselves. There are rapists roving about
in society seeking to seize man's personness and carry it
off by force. Somebody needs to scream *rape!*

How you value your self is most critical, because *your
self-esteem is all you've got*. Most of the models of man are
destructive, because they will devalue your self.

Man—Nothing But Molecules?

The particular rapist I'm referring to carries man's personness off by minimizing the explanation of his parts. In
other words, man is just a collection of molecules.

To the chemist, man is a compilation of chemicals, quite ordinary elements with familiar properties—well-behaved molecules combining regularly and predictably. Some of the combinations are highly complex, but gradually the fascinating story has been told of amino acids, proteins, enzymes, and even the DNA. In 1953 Drs. Francis Crick and James D. Watson announced their discoveries of these intricate molecules that transmit genetic characteristics. Blue eyes, fair hair, and even the talent for mathematics can all be traced to the nucleic acids on the DNA strands. The miracles of blood, muscle, and nerve can all be reduced to ordered patterns of biochemical laws. Man is a collection of common chemicals—mostly carbon, with a dash of phosphorus, enough iron to make a six-inch nail, and enough sulphur to rid one dog of fleas—put together with about a hundredweight of water.[1]

But where is "man" in this collection of molecules? His molecules change completely every seven years or so—yours are changing in part even as you read this page—so how is personness, your *self*, related to this changing molecular pile?[2]

One of the major problems with this rapist is that *meaning* is left out of the cold, impersonal, chemical explanation. The British scientist and philosopher Donald McKay cleverly illustrates this with a neon sign. We can understand the principles of a neon sign—how the filaments work, how the current goes through, how the atoms are broken down into electrons with positive ions going in opposite directions to maintain the beautiful colors—perfectly well without realizing that what it says is Joe's Bar and Grill. The meaning of the sign is not reducible to the physical chemistry of the neon tubes. Likewise, the meaning of this sentence is not reducible to its letters, even though the letters make up 100 percent of its content.[3]

Is that all man is—a collection of molecules or a chemical reaction?

Man—Nothing But a Machine?

This rapist says man is only a product of his environment. He's just a stimulus-response machine with no trace of personness.

B. F. Skinner, the famous Harvard psychologist, and his followers advocate that man is a product of his surroundings. His behavior is in no way a result of his own decisions or desires, but is totally determined by his outside world. The behaviorists believe humans are subjects who can be molded at will to a particular pattern of behavior. Like the laboratory animals, they can be conditioned by Skinner's method of reward.

The behaviorists do away with man as a unique creative being, with his inner person. As Skinner says: "What is being abolished is autonomous man—the inner man . . . the man defended by the literatures of freedom and dignity. His abolition has long been overdue. . . . To man as man we readily say good riddance."[4]

Man becomes part of the cosmic machinery! Everything he is, everything he makes, everything he thinks is completely, 100 percent, determined by his environment. "Man" doesn't exist—he's just not there. All that's there is a bundle of conditioning, a genetic code, the past, and the environment. Man is nothing but a machine—raped of his personness![5]

Man—Nothing But an Animal?

Man is raped again! This time unique personness is carried off by reducing him to a biological organism. Undoubtedly he is the best developed of the animals, but he is still a physiological specimen whose primary function is to survive and reproduce.

As did the first two rapists, this one has also left an indelible mark on how we value ourselves. In the 1960s three or four books were published which assumed that the "real" human nature would be found by examining animal and bird behavior. The "naked ape" is "inescapably hostile and competitive," they said, and even his friendships and loves are rooted in an animalistic aggression and territory defense. Anthony Storr really laid it on thick in the introduction to his book *Human Aggression* (which he dedicated to Konrad Lorenz with "admiration and affection," qualities that must have temporarily outweighed his aggression):

> That man is an aggressive creature will hardly be disputed . . . the cruellest and most ruthless species that has ever walked the earth; and that, although we may recoil in horror when we read in newspaper or history book of the atrocities committed by man upon man, we know in our hearts that each one of us harbors within himself those same savage impulses which lead to murder, to torture and to war.

There is more than suggestion in all this that aggression, like sexual impulse, is built into the biological structure of humanity, and there is little that can be done about it.[6]

Is man just the apex of the evolutionary process? Is he nothing but an animal? People have been taught this for so long that much of the time they act like animals toward other "animals."

Man = Impersonal Origin + Time + Chance

Man has been raped and left for dead! He becomes simply the product of an impersonal origin with only the addition of the equally impersonal time and chance. He has a genetic code, and he has an environment to shape the product of the code. But that's all he has, and all he is. Man is dead![7]

It's interesting to note the way the rapists of personness inject personness back into their non-person systems. Dr. Francis Crick says, "You cannot lay down a general trend (for the course of evolution); natural selection is *cleverer* than that. It will *think* of combinations and ways of doing things which haven't been foreseen" (italics mine). Crick's language here attributes to natural selection a sort of personality. In the *Origin of the Genetic Code* (1967) he calls nature a "she." In other words he personalizes what his own system has defined as impersonal. He does so because he can't stand the implications of impersonality, and this kind of semantic mysticism gives relief to people caught in the web of the impersonal.[8]

Man can't live within the impersonal systems for one very simple reason—his own personness. Personness just doesn't fit within the impersonal. It's like a fish attempting to live out of water or a train maneuvering through a field without a set of tracks. It just doesn't fit!

Man is a collection of molecules, a stimulus-response machine, and highly developed animal, but he is not *only* any one of these or only a combination of these. Man is something more. When he views himself as just molecules, a machine, or an animal, he becomes extremely frustrated, and dissatisfaction sets in on the gut level. To avoid being forced into the impersonal mode, which would mean death to him as a man, he then starts striking out against his nature. If man is in an impersonal universe, then the things that make him man—love, hope, rationality, morality, creativity, communication, and choice— are unfulfillable and therefore meaningless. Man becomes as dead as a fish out of water and as meaningless as a train without a set of tracks.

When facing the desperate problems you must face in your life, can you understand how difficult it is to move into recovery from them. If you start out with the given that you have been raped of your personness—your *self*— you don't have much of a chance. Your security, social, and significance needs will never be met beginning from this base. Where is the value, the esteem, if you can't even recover the self?

Plan: Mark of God on Man

Your self-esteem, including your security, social, and significance needs—your personness—must be built on an adequate base of reality. This base must be strong enough to support all you are and secure enough so you can't fall off. What you need is a floor. You can fall off walls, balconies, buildings, swings, bridges, cliffs, or out of the air, but you can't fall off the floor! You must have a realistic base. I'm convinced this realistic base can only come from what I call the *mark of God on man*.

The more I work with the problem of self-esteem, the more I realize how crucial the mark of your Creator is to your value. It's no different when it comes to any work of art. If I offer you two paintings, a work by Remington and a work by Timmons, each for the same price, there will be no question in your mind which is more valuable. The reason? There is only one reason for this. The creator of the painting! The same is true with viewing God as your

Creator. There are, at least, three ways to look at your creation:

1. Man came from nothing.
2. Man came from impersonal.
3. Man came from personal.

Man Came From Nothing

The first possibility is that all existence came out of nothing. Now, to hold this view, it must be *absolutely* nothing. It can't be nothing something or something nothing. It must be nothing nothing, which means there must be no energy, no mass, no motion, and *no personality*. Practically, this option is unthinkable. But theoretically, it's the first possible answer.[9]

Man Came From Impersonal

The second possibility is that all existence came from an impersonal beginning. The impersonality could be mass, energy, motion, or a combination of things, but they would all be equally impersonal. If an impersonal beginning is accepted, some form of reductionism always follows. Everything, from the stars to man himself, is finally understood by reducing it to the original, impersonal factor or factors—just mass, energy, motion, or whatever.[10]

The biggest problem in beginning with the impersonal is to find meaning for the particulars. If we begin with the impersonal, then how do any of the particulars now existing—including man—have any meaning, any significance? Beginning with the impersonal, everything, including man, must be explained in terms of the impersonal plus time plus chance.[11]

The impersonal base is commonly called *naturalism*. Naturalism holds that everything can be explained by the natural laws of the universe. All existence and its operation is confined to this closed system, and nothing exists or operates outside of it. In other words, all existence is one big cosmic machine, and it includes people as they are. Man finds himself caught in it—in fact, he is only a cog in the machine.

Naturalism is the base for humanism, and humanism is the base for the bankruptcy of personness. The dilemma of modern humanism and the reason for the declaration of bankruptcy is simple. It's matter plus time plus chance equals zero. If man is the illegitimate offspring of a thoughtless parent order, the mockery of fortuitous chance, his significance is nil—zero! Add to this man's inhumanity to man, and the dilemma is intensified. As the humanist is faced with this, his dreams come to wreckage and ruin, and his hopes for a utopian future are shattered.

There isn't an exit from the closed system of naturalism, from the dilemma of humanism. Even man's gods are part of the closed system and therefore incapable of an adequate base for providing personness. There is no way out. Life quickly becomes a dead-end street.

Man Came From Personal

The third possibility is that all existence came from a *personal* beginning. With a personal beginning as well as the impersonal beginning everything happens according to the natural laws of the universe. But instead of it happening in a closed system (naturalism), it happens in an open system (supernaturalism). In other words, all existence isn't one big cosmic machine, and people as they are don't have to be included in it. In an open system, there is something "outside" the cosmic machinery—outside the uniformity of the natural laws—something *super*natural. This "something" outside the natural system is normally called God, your Creator. Because supernaturalism is an open and personal system, God becomes an adequate base for creating personness—because He Himself is personal.

Within this supernatural yet personal beginning there is hope! Things go on according to the sequence of natural laws, but at any point in time they may be changed by God or by people. This supernatural, personal beginning is an adequate base for personness—for your security, social, and significance needs. It's the only adequate base for valuing and esteeming your self!

The Munich comedian Karl Vallentin was famous for a skit that illustrates the futility of man's search for answers to life. Coming onto the stage in almost total darkness, with one solitary circle of light provided by a street lamp, he paced around and around looking for something. Soon a policeman crossed the stage and asked him what he had lost. Vallentin answered that he had lost the key to his house. The policeman joined in the hunt, but after a while the search appeared fruitless. "Are you sure you lost it here?" asked the policeman. "Oh, no!" said Vallentin, pointing to the dark corner. "I lost it over there." "Then why on earth are you looking over here?" asked the policeman. "Because there's no light over there!" replied Vallentin.

The rape of personness forces man to search for meaning in a small lighted area where there is no answer. You see, your self-esteem is all you've got. Your self-esteem is *you!* God as your Creator wants to be your Partner in the business of self-esteem; turn Him down and you're out of business!

14
I'm Not OK, You're Not OK, But That's OK

I once read an interesting piece of graffiti on a restroom wall. It was a picture of a radio with a message coming out of the speaker. The message said: "This life is a test. It is only a test. Had this been an actual life, you would have received instructions as to what to do and where to go." Wouldn't it be great if that were really the case? I'd have time to make a few mistakes and still cram for the real thing.

Well, if you were starting to get a little excited, let me carefully set the record straight. This life is definitely *not* a test for the real thing later. This *is* the real thing—today! Now, I know what you're thinking. *OK then, if this is it, where are the directions?* We have been walking through the Twelve Steps toward your personal recovery and discovery. Now, let's get on with the summary of life's directions.

OK or Not OK?

For years I have loved the statement "I don't fear my life will come to an end, but I fear my life may not have a beginning." All of us have this yearning inside to do something with our lives that counts for something. And in order to make our lives count, we must start somewhere—we must *begin*. This is the most difficult place to be in life. Yet it's the getting started that sometimes makes all the difference.

There is a foundational teaching throughout the Bible that defines the best way to begin. The central theme of each of these teachings is *humility*. Humility has two meanings. It is the opposite of pride, but it is also a right evaluation of who you are. It's the true evaluation of yourself—the good and the bad—the up side and the down side.

Let's look at the up side first. The up side of man is that there is a wonder about him. You are not a rock, not a plant, not an animal; you are a unique human being. You are a person who can love, hope, reason, create, communicate, make choices, and possess a sense of morality. You are an unrepeatable miracle! You are truly wonderful! But that's not the whole picture.

The down side of man is that there is also a wickedness about him. Freud taught this concept as a basic tenet of his system. You are wonderful, but not totally, because there is a basic wickedness inside that makes you capable of doing anything, anyplace, anytime! It is always a shock when we read about atrocities in the newspaper; man's inhumanity to other men is hard to comprehend. Yet, if it were not for the grace of God, you and I could easily be committing the exact same (or worse) crime or atrocity. You are not as bad as you could be, but you are truly wicked!

You must be very careful to view both of these in a balanced perspective. If you concentrate upon the wonder of man alone, you will think you can be perfect only to be caught by surprise when your wicked side flares up! And if you concentrate upon the wickedness of man alone, you will personally try to beat the devil out of your kids or you'll be in a perpetual state of depression over how bad you really are. The wonder and the wickedness of man must be viewed in balance—both must be considered together. There is a wonder about me which makes me grateful, but there is a wickedness about me which sometimes makes me groan. There is a wonder about me which I must cultivate, but there is a wickedness about me which I must learn to control. Considering them both at once paints the picture of true humility!

This picture is what brought me to a whole new understanding of the most healthy beginning point of life. We all wanted to believe the popular book title *I'm OK, You're OK!* But this theme only presented half of the true human picture. It suddenly occurred to me one morning years ago that the most accurate way to put it was, I'm not OK, you're not OK, but that's OK! because there is a wonder about me and a wonder about you that gives me hope as I work on my OK-ness!

This has become a major theme in our church. I frequently say to our congregation, "Our church is only for people who don't have it together. If you feel you have it together, you may be more comfortable elsewhere." Teasingly, I stress that there is no one here who has it together with the possible exception of the senior pastor—me! This theme is not just a cute theme, but a powerful attitude that draws people into the church. We have experienced a steady growth for over nine years from 400 to over 10,000 people. All of the growth is by word of mouth and approximately 100 to 130 new families are visiting each week. I'm convinced that a major factor in our growth is this basic, balanced attitude.

Begin Where You Lack

The ultimate benefit you will gain from this attitudinal balance is the setup for significant, personal growth. It's at this point that we turn back to one of the central themes of the Bible: The best beginning is to start where you lack. Jehovah, the God of Israel, called on His people to "humble" themselves, "repent" of their pride in sackcloth and ashes, and to "cleanse" themselves from their wicked and selfish ways.

Jesus made it clear that He came as a Physician to heal the sick. In other words, if you don't recognize your sickness—where you lack—you will not be healed or significantly touched by the Physician. This is precisely why Jesus attacked the religious leadership of His day. They thought they had it together. Their hypocritical piousness was a major obstacle to admitting their need for a healing touch from the Lord.

In the Sermon on the Mount (Matthew 5–7) Jesus walks into the Beatitudes with, "Blessed are the poor in spirit . . . Blessed are those who mourn . . . Blessed are the meek . . . Blessed are those who hunger and thirst for righteousness." The *poor in spirit*, not the rich and healthy in spirit. The *mourners*, not those who are applauding, cheering, and reveling. The *meek*, not the boisterous or the strong-willed. The ones who are *hungering and thirsting*, not those who are filled and satisfied already.

When you examine the ministry of Jesus, you will discover that He did His best work with those who humbly presented themselves and their needs to Him. This is the way He works best! God does His best work in the midst of death and dying and where life is filled with pain and problems.

The Apostle Paul, in his letter to the church at Corinth, says that through our inadequacies and weaknesses God's adequacy and strengths become most evident! James writes, "God will draw near to the humble, but resists the proud."

In fact, God is so into this principle as the best way of dealing with people and their recovery process, that He'll do anything it takes to get you into that proper place of beginning. He says, "He who humbles himself will be exalted. And he who exalts himself will be humbled." Although I can't say that I have ever enjoyed it, I know that I seem to have growth spurts in my life only when I have to face pain and problems—the death and the dying. If you want to experience true recovery, you must begin right where you lack.

After the Beginning—Now What?

Now that you know the most effective beginning point, how do you get on with living life most successfully? Whether it be in the professional areas of counseling, communicating, selling, managing, and administrating or in the personal areas of self-esteem, marriage, parenthood, and friendships, the answer to living life most successfully includes the same three dynamic processes—*becoming, relating,* and *achieving.* I want to consider these processes in reverse order.

Process of Achieving—Responsibility

The first is the process of achieving. This is the area of your life which most closely affects what you do with your life. The goal of the process of achieving is to have impact—to make your mark—to do something worth- while! This relates to the need for significance that we referred to earlier.

The primary theme is responsibility. Responsibility is a lost art; there's a responsibility crisis going on in our world. No one seems to be responsible in anything, and an enormous amount of energy is exerted in trying to place the blame elsewhere. A little rhyme illustrates this: "The person who can smile when things go wrong has thought of someone to blame it on!"

Two extremes exist in the responsibility crisis. The first is *irresponsibility*. This is when you're not accepting per- sonal responsibility at all for your actions, but tend to blame other people or circumstances. The other extreme is *overresponsibility*. This is when you feel responsible for ev- erything and everyone. The deceiving thing about this last extreme is you *are* responsible for some things (not all, only some), but you are *not* responsible for other people! The problem with being responsible for other people (whether they be family or friends) is you inevitably re- lieve them from responsibility altogether. This may be why some children are resistant, and even shocked, when their parents expect responsibility from them. Since their par- ents have always been responsible for them, why do the children need to be concerned about responsibility! The trick here is for parents to gradually move from being responsible *for* their children to being responsible *to* their children as they grow up.

You and only you are responsible for your *self*. And you are responsible to your world. Now, having said that, it's important to point out a couple of depressing thoughts. First, no one is as excited about what you are doing as you are. No one! Go ahead, try it out. Ask people if they're

excited about what you're doing. You'll receive a full spectrum of responses from a yawn to tacit approval to rejection. Nobody cares as much about what you are doing as
you do.

Now, if you thought that was depressing, then this second truth may push you across the line of despair: There
is no meeting going on right now to discuss how to make
your day! Oh, there may be a meeting and they may even
be talking about you, but their stated purpose is *not* to
make your life wonderful!

In evaluating these two depressing thoughts the bottom
line is that if anything positive is going to happen in your
life, *you* must make it happen! You must take personal
responsibility for your life and how it's lived out. Now,
don't misunderstand me here. I'm not suggesting that you
ignore God's grace or work in your life. But you must do
the possible, by faith that God will do the impossible.

God's role in your life doesn't diminish your responsibility in any way.

There was a farmer who had planted and cultivated a
garden in back of his house. He had worked very hard to
turn a dismal piece of dirt into a lush garden full of all sorts
of vegetation. He invited his priest out to see this beautiful
sight. As the priest walked through the garden he exclaimed, "Look what God has done here. God can really
grow corn, can't He? Look at those tomatoes God has
grown over there!" The more the priest went on about
God's incredible role in this garden, the angrier the farmer
became at his priest's utter disregard for what he, the
farmer, had done in this project. When he could take no
more, he yelled out at the priest, "Father, you should have
seen this garden when God was doing it by Himself!"

You do the possible, by faith that God will do the impossible. Just as God majors in the impossible, you must

major in the possible. You must learn to be personally responsible for your life. This is the process of achieving.

There's one caution here: Beware of the It Trap we talked about back in chapter 4. Remember, no matter what, when you finally get to it, somebody took it—*it* is gone! You see, there is no arrival point in life, but you are always in process.

Process of Relating—Relationship

The second process is that of relating. This is the area of your life which reflects whom you will associate with in life. The goal of relating is to experience intimacy—interdependence with other human beings. Naturally, the theme in this process is relationship which relates to the social needs mentioned earlier.

On the whole, people are good at surfacey relationships. "How are you? How's your job, family, car, health?" But most people are not very effective in developing intimate relationships.

There is something about relationships that is significantly powerful in how it affects your whole being. The process of achieving is either boosted or dragged down by how your relationships are going. How you feel personally is also greatly affected by how well your relationships are going.

There's no better place to work on relationships than in your personal life—with your mate or a significant other. I've come to realize over the years that the two basic types of people—male and female—are extremely different. In fact, after long and studied observation, I've determined that women are weird and men are very strange! Without this perspective your relationships are already in trouble. Allow me to illustrate what I mean.

Women and men are very different. When a party invitation is received, what is each one's response? The woman says, "What shall I wear?" The man says, "How can I get out of this one?"

A woman says to her man, "Do you love me?" "You do, don't you?" "How much do you love me?" "Do you love me as much as you used to?" The man is thinking, *I told you I loved you when I married you. It's still in effect until I take it back!* Men and women are different!

Since men and women are so different, you must learn to be a student of your intimate relationships. You must learn what makes your loved one *tick* or *ticked!*

Not only are your most intimate loved ones crucial in the process of relating, but so are your friends and your extended family. There is something almost supernaturally dynamic about a warm, open, supportive relationship that must be a part of your game plan for recovery and discovery.

Take the time to cultivate your relationships. No, *make* the time for your relationships. No, better yet, *invest* in your relationships.

Process of Becoming—Reality

The third process is the process of becoming. This is the area of your life that reflects *who* you are becoming. The goal of the process of becoming is to discover your identity. This is the most crucial dynamic of all. You are the most important ingredient to all of the equations you are attempting to put together. The you that you take into relationships will greatly affect those relationships and your intimacy. The you that you take into the process of achieving will ultimately determine your success or failure.

The theme of the process of becoming is *reality*. Now, no

one really likes reality. I recently saw a bumper sticker that read "Reality is only for those who can't cope with drugs!"

I've noticed there are two extreme ways of defining reality. One group says life is always being on top of the pile—filled with optimism—positive, with rarely a thought of the negative. When asked, "How are you?" people in this group will say, "Super! Fantastic! Couldn't be better!" (Outside they may be smiling, on the inside they may be dying.) You get the suspicious feeling they must be smoking something in order to be on top of the pile all the time! In this extreme you have to be on top of the pile all the time—exciting everyone, all the time, about life.

The other group says life is always being underneath the pile—filled with pessimism—always dwelling on the negative, with rarely a thought of the positive. "Life is getting worse," warn those in this extreme, "and it probably won't get any better. You'd better come with us to the next life. It will be better there—at least we hope so." People in this group have faces long enough to eat popcorn out of a milk bottle! Instead of exciting people about life (as do those who are on top of the pile), they're embalming people—preparing everyone for an early death!

Both of these extremes are wrong! Reality isn't being on top of the pile all the time or underneath the pile all the time. Let me give you reality: Life is full of piles! Don't try to ignore it or deny it or sugarcoat it! The position in which you find yourself with life's onslaught is always changing. You may be on top of the pile or underneath. You may be trying to go around the pile or attempting to shovel through. The object of life is to get through the piles!

The process of achieving focuses upon your significance needs, the process of relating focuses upon your social needs, and the process of becoming focuses upon your security needs. As I attempted to point out earlier in this book, your security needs ultimately must be met through your spiritual journey. In other words, as you search for true, personal security you must find it in your search for God! I'm learning that everyone—atheists (who believe in no God), agnostics (who don't know if there is a God), and theists (who believe in God)—is on a spiritual journey. The main difference is where each one is along the way.

Get One Watch

In the process of becoming, you must search for a realistic base for living your life. There's a terrific adage that says "If you have one watch, you know what time it is! If you have two, you are never sure!" Most people have several different watches in order to tell them what time it is—one for their social life, one for their family life, another for their business life, and still another for their personal life. It's no surprise that we are living in a moral/ethical crisis today. No one knows what time it is!

I have found the one watch that offers me a realistic base for life as it is and people as they are—the Bible! Now, I feel a little like the Toyota commercial that says, "If you can find a better car than Toyota, buy it!" I say, "If you can find a better base than I've found, then buy it!" But you must find a realistic base that tells you what time it is (a value system for living out your life).

On a flight from New York to Los Angeles, an executive sat down beside me. After a few conversational clichés, he asked, "What do you do?"

I quickly replied, "I speak."

He said, "I know that, but what do you do for a living?"

Again I said, "I speak!"

"On what?" he continued.

"Well, I speak on life-style, marriage, parenting, long-term selling and managing, and so on."

He seemed impressed. "Really! Are you a psychiatrist?"

"No," I replied, "but I have a psychiatrist who works with me."

"Well then," he said, "are you a psychologist?"

"No, I'm not one of those either, but I do have two of them who work for me."

Then in a somewhat frustrated manner, he said, "Well, what are you?" Now it hurts a little bit when someone asks, "*What* are you?" but I bounced back with, "I'm just a speaker." Now that my profession was established, he started on his second set of twenty questions.

"Where do you get your material?"

I told him he probably wouldn't believe it if I told him.

"No," he said, "come on, where do you get your stuff?"

So I told him, "I get it out of a book."

"In a book! What's the title of the book?" he asked.

I had him get ready to write down the title of my resource book.

Calmly I announced, "The title of the book is Bible."

He seemed a little stunned with my answer and said in a rather loud voice, "Bible! You get your material to speak to corporations from the Bible? What is there to talk about in the Bible?"

I'd observed a couple of nudie magazines in his briefcase earlier, so I knew what would get his attention. So I said, "I speak quite a bit on sex!"

He choked slightly and said, "From the Bible?" His shock came from a common misconception that the Bible says, "Thou shalt not!" about sex. It actually says, "Thou shalt!" and it even goes so far as to say, "Thou shalt enjoy it when thou shalt!"

"Oh, yes, from the Bible!" I assured him. "There are all kinds of principles concerning sex in the Bible! Moses wrote in Deuteronomy 24:5 that when a man gets married, he shouldn't be drafted into the military or work for the first year, but he should *cheer up* his wife for a year! I can't explain it all right now, but the Hebrew word for 'cheer up' doesn't mean to tell jokes for a year. It's referring to sex!"

Now he began to take notes. "Now, where did you say that verse was?" Can't you just see him going to his hotel room and pulling out the Gideon Bible from the nightstand drawer!

The Bible offers a realistic base for living life most successfully. It's true to life as it really is and people as they really are. If you can find a better base than I have found, you better buy it!

In this book I have offered you a game plan for living a successful life on purpose—realistically, relationally, and responsibly! Use this game plan as a tool for processing your own life and for making a difference in the world of people all around you who are hurting.

I think Snoopy, that great psychologist of the twentieth century, put it best when he said, "It doesn't really make a difference whether you win or you lose—until you lose! And then it makes a difference!" Learn to win in the game of life through this simple and practical game plan. Do it now—this life is not a test, it's the real thing!

For information on additional tools to help you develop your own personal game plan for living contact:

Game Plan for Living
P.O. Box 2200
Orange, CA 92669
714–974-1431

Source Notes

Chapter 1: Problems and Pain

1. Melody Beattie, *Codependent No More* (New York: Harper & Row, 1987), p. 31.
2. Earnie Larsen, quoted in Beattie, *Codependent No More*, p. 28.
3. Beattie, *Codependent No More*, pp. 33, 34.
4. John Powell, S. J., *Why Am I Afraid to Love* (Valencia, Calif.: Tabor Publishing, 1972), p. 59.

Chapter 5: Moral Surgery

1. Ann Landi, "When Having Everything Isn't Enough," *Psychology Today* (April 1989), p. 28.

Chapter 8: How High Is Your Higher Power?

1. W. F. Albright, *Archaeology and the Religion of Israel* (Baltimore: Johns Hopkins, 1942), p. 176.
2. Sir Frederic Kenyon, *The Bible and Archaeology* (New York: Harper and Brothers, 1940), p. 279.
3. Sir W. M. Ramsay, *The Bearing of Recent Discovery on the Trustworthiness of the New Tes-*

tament (London: Hodder and Stoughton, 1915), p. 222.

4. Sir Frederic Kenyon, *Our Bible and the Ancient Manuscripts* (New York: Harper and Brothers, 1941), p. 23.

5. Ibid., p. 23.

6. Norman L. Geisler and William E. Nix, *A General Introduction to the Bible* (Chicago: Moody, 1968, 1986), p. 365.

7. Ibid., p. 263.

8. Prophecy: Micah 5:2; Fulfillment: Matthew 2:1.

9. Prophecy: Isaiah 40:3; Fulfillment: Matthew 3:1, 2.

10. Prophecy: Zechariah 9:9; Fulfillment Luke 19:35–37a.

11. Prophecy: Psalm 41:9; Fulfillment: Matthew 10:4.

12. Prophecy: Zechariah 11:12; Fulfillment: Matthew 26:15.

13. Prophecy: Zechariah 11:13b; Fulfillment: Matthew 27:5a.

14. Prophecy: Isaiah 53:7; Fulfillment: Matthew 27:12–19.

15. Prophecy: Psalm 22:16; Fulfillment: Luke 23:33.

16. Prophecy: Isaiah 53:12; Fulfillment: Matthew 27:38.

17. Peter W. Stoner, *Science Speaks* (Chicago: Moody, 1958, 1963, 1968), pp. 100–107.

18. Robert Anderson, *The Coming Prince* (Grand Rapids: Kregel, 1975), p. 127.

19. John 14:10 AT.

20. John 14:9 AT.

21. John 8:19 AT.
22. Mark 9:37 AT.
23. John 5:23 AT.
24. Frank Mead, ed., *The Encyclopedia of Religious Quotations* (Old Tappan, N.J.: Fleming H. Revell Company, n.d.), p. 50.
25. C. S. Lewis, *Mere Christianity* (New York: Macmillan, 1943), p. 56.
26. Mead, *Encyclopedia of Religious Quotations*, p. 56.

Chapter 13: Your Self-Esteem Is All You've Got

1. Charles Martin, *How Human Can You Get?* (Downers Grove, Ill.: Inter-Varsity Press, 1973), pp. 16, 17.
2. Ibid., p. 18.
3. David Myers, *The Human Puzzle* (New York: Harper and Row, 1978), p. 13.
4. Francis Schaeffer, *Back to Freedom and Dignity* (Downers Grove, Ill.: Inter-Varsity Press, 1972), p. 33.
5. Ibid., pp. 34, 35.
6. Charles Martin, *How Human Can You Get?* pp. 29, 30.
7. Francis Schaeffer, *Back to Freedom and Dignity*, pp. 19, 20.
8. Ibid., p. 18.
9. Francis Schaeffer, *He Is There and He Is Not Silent* (Wheaton, Ill.: Tyndale House, 1972), p. 7.
10. Ibid., p. 8.
11. Ibid., pp. 8, 9.